AMOS AND HIS MESSAGE

AMOS

AND HIS
MESSAGE

AN EXPOSITORY COMMENTARY

Roy L. Honeycutt

BROADMAN PRESS • Nashville, Tennessee

All Scripture references unless otherwise noted are
either from the *Revised Standard Version of the Bible,*
copyrighted 1946 and 1952, or are the author's original
translation.

421-075

02326626

DEWEY DECIMAL CLASSIFICATION: 224.8

Library of Congress catalog card number: 63-19071

Printed in the United States of America

4.JUL6313

To

my wife

June

(Ruth 1:16-17)

Preface

God's presence was as certain for the prophets as was the echo of a lion's roar along the rocky crags of the wilderness. As a prophet, Amos labored under the impetus of such an impelling conviction of divine-human encounter. For him and for his generation, the Lion had roared! Yahweh, the Lord of history, had hurled his word into the arena of human encounter, once again calling all men into conflict.

AMOS AND HIS MESSAGE has been written with the sincere desire to capture this same note. Designed as an expository commentary, the primary purpose of the book is to utilize the benefits of technical study in order to confront this generation with the roar of the Lion. However, it is not with the purpose of listening to the *echo* of the roar that the present work has been produced. Rather, it is with the hope that through this effort the actual voice of God will be heard, arising newborn out of a personal encounter with him because of the study of Holy Scripture.

I would not only be remiss in responsibility, but ungrateful as well, if I did not give credit to three men, especially, who have been responsible for the deepening of my own understanding of the Old Testament. I am particularly indebted to Dr. J. J. Owens in the area of linguistic studies. I am grateful for the warmth and cordiality of his friendship over many years. Dr. W. H. Morton, former professor and present colleague, through the medium of biblical archaeology introduced me to the life situation of the Old Testament. The depth of his own apprehension of the biblical revelation has been both an inspiration and a stimulant to further understanding. A debt of special gratitude should be expressed also to Dr. Clyde T. Francisco, who, in an elective on the minor

prophets, caused the prophets to come alive with a note of relevance that I had never before discerned. While due credit should
be expressed to him for the stimulation of many ideas in the study
of Amos, I would not assess him with the liability of my personal
judgments and approach. I do, however, gladly acknowledge his
contribution to my life and to my attitude toward the relevance
of the Old Testament to contemporary life.

I am also indebted to all of my colleagues on the faculty of
Midwestern Baptist Theological Seminary. Especially to Dr. J.
Morris Ashcraft, who read the typescript, and to Dr. William
Coble, who read the proofs, I express appreciation. The encouragement and counsel of Dr. H. I. Hester, vice-president of Midwestern Seminary, has been cordially appreciated. To the president
of the seminary, Dr. Millard J. Berquist, there is an indebtedness
which is all but incalculable. The adequate physical provisions
made possible through his leadership have made both research and
writing not only a possibility but a joy. Beyond this, however, his
sympathetic concern for the cultivation of an atmosphere con-
ducive to progressive theological education continues to make
possible the total ministry of a seminary professor.

There is also a debt of gratitude which is almost incapable
of expression that I would, nonetheless, attempt to make concrete.
For I am indebted to a host of people throughout the Southern
Baptist Convention who made possible a theological education at
the Southern Baptist Theological Seminary, and who continue to
make possible the opportunity for such research and writing as
that reflected in AMOS AND HIS MESSAGE. For the support of these
men and women whose faces I have never seen, whose voices I
have never heard, but whose provisions I daily utilize, I am deeply
and sincerely appreciative.

ROY L. HONEYCUTT

Contents

1

From Tekoa to Samaria

Up from the bleak hills of Tekoa came this
  Shepherd turned prophet by the voice of God's roar;
Up from the life so familiar with terror,
  So filled with oppression and so fraught with injustice.
Up from the southland came this prophet of old,
  Sunbronzed and hardened, mature and emboldened.
Up came this prophet at the command of his God,
  To rebuke and accuse, to attack and condemn.
Up came this prophet at the roar of the Lion,
  A man under God for a world under sin!

With the voice of God still echoing the roar of the prophetic
call, Amos came upward from Judah to Israel. The Lion had,
indeed, roared; who could do other than prophesy? The prophet's
penetrating insight and clear perception had isolated the ultimate
cause for the degenerate social structures of the day. With courage born of a fearless occupation and bred of a direct encounter
with God, Amos gave expression to the convictions which were his
through the revelation of God.

Respected across the years, Amos rightly deserves the praise
often ascribed to him. In this regard, no greater anthology of
praise has ever been collected for the prophet than that by Knudson, who introduces it by saying, "A century ago he was simply
one of the minor prophets. No special significance attached to
him . . . but observe what the pillars of Old Testament scholarship now say." [1]

---

[1] A. C. Knudson, *The Beacon Lights of Prophecy* (New York: The Methodist Book Concern, 1914), p. 57.

1

"The book of Amos," says *Cheyne,* "forms a literary as well as a prophetic phenomenon." "To the unprejudiced judgment," says *W. Robertson Smith,* "the prophecy of Amos appears as one of the best examples of pure Hebrew style. The language, the images, the grouping are
alike admirable; and the simplicity of the diction . . . is a token, not of
rusticity, but of perfect mastery." "There is nowhere," says *Harper,* "to
be found in the Old Testament an example of a stronger or purer literary
style." "His language," says *Driver,* "is pure, his style classical and re-
fined." . . . *Wellhausen* says that he was "the founder of the purest type
of a new phase of prophecy." *Marti* declares that he is "one of the most
prominent landmarks in the history of religion." *Kuenen* speaks of him
and his immediate successors as "the creators of ethical monotheism,"
and *Cornill* describes him as "one of the most marvelous and incom-
prehensible figures in the history of the human mind, the pioneer of a
process of evolution from which a new epoch of humanity dates."[2]

The shadow of a man is shaped not only by the man, but also
by the surface on which it falls.[3] The surface on which Amos
stood must, therefore, be examined in order to understand his
lengthening shadow. One must consider not only the religious factors
of the day, but also the historical and social circumstances surrounding the prophet. Each of these did much to shape the form of Amos'
shadow or message.

Amos: The Man

While Amos worked no miracles himself, he has been declared
by at least one writer to have been "a living miracle." [4] Even this
extreme evaluation of the prophet's influence does not exceed the
bounds of reality. He was from numerous points of view a miracle
of God. That human personality could be so infused with the
divine spirit as to cause one to arise in spite of the adversities
of the eighth century was all but unbelievable. That a man from
Tekoa, a shepherd and a fruit picker, should become the medium
of divine revelation can only be called a miracle. Numerous facets
of both his times and his personality must be clarified if one is
to understand this "miracle."

[2] *Ibid.,* pp. 56-57. Italics are the author's.
[3] S. H. Blank, *Prophetic Faith in Isaiah* (New York: Harper & Brothers,
1958), p. 9.
[4] W. R. Harper, *A Critical and Exegetical Commentary on Amos and Hosea*
("The International Critical Commentary," eds. Samuel Driver, Alfred Plum-
mer, and Charles Briggs [Edinburgh: T. & T. Clark, 1905]), p. cvi.

The times in which Amos lived.—A recent Old Testament scholar has observed that a man cannot exist in a vacuum, much less prophesy in one. Consequently, "the prophet, like the poet, must know the throb and thrill of a real experience before he has anything to interpret; his soul needs the stimulus of national and international life around him." [5] Because of this twofold relationship between historic actualities and human personality, it is imperative that any consideration of Amos be preceded by a study of the political, social, and religious matrix that gave birth to the prophet.

Politically, Amos lived in a time of relative peace on the international scene. The two major areas of international influence, Egypt and Assyria, were both in a period of decline, although Assyria was beginning a new advance. The lesser power of Syria had finally been reduced to a state of ineffective opposition to Israel. However, the reduction of this buffer state between Israel and Assyria was to have serious repercussions for Israel within the generation following Amos. In the context of this political vacuum on the international scene, Israel entered into an era of peace during the second quarter of the eighth century such as she had not known for at least a full century.

Internally, the political structure of both Israel and Judah was one of stability. Beginning his prophetic ministry during the reign of Jeroboam II, Amos prophesied during an era that rivaled that of Solomon. Although condemned on religious grounds by the Deuteronomic editor of the book of Kings, Jeroboam's forty-one-year reign politically represented an island of stability in a vast sea of rampant governmental insecurity (2 Kings 14:23-24). Geographically, Jeroboam II extended the borders of Israel to include the largest area the Northern Kingdom ever controlled. Economically, he led Israel into a golden era of prosperity. The very length and stability of Jeroboam's reign speaks much concerning the force of his personality and influence.

While Jeroboam II reigned in Israel, Uzziah reigned in Judah. Amos dated his ministry during the era of this stalwart king (cf. 1:1). Under Uzziah's able leadership, the Philistines and the Ara-

---

[5] H. Wheeler Robinson, *The Cross in the Old Testament* (London: SCM Press, 1955), p. 137.

bians were conquered, Eloth was built, and tribute was exacted from the Ammonites. Jerusalem was also fortified and a great army was organized (2 Chron. 26:1-15).[6]

But more specifically, at exactly what point during the reign of Jeroboam and Uzziah did Amos prophesy? The prophet dated his call "two years before the earthquake." It appears that such an earthquake may have accompanied a total eclipse of the sun on June 15, 763 B.C.[7] If this was the case, then Amos' call would have occurred two years earlier in 765 B.C. (1:1). Amos knew nothing of the period of anarchy that followed the death of Jeroboam II and consequently must have ended his ministry prior to *ca.* 750 B.C., the terminal point for the reign of Jeroboam II (cf. 2 Kings 15:8-15). It was within this fifteen-year period that the prophet's contribution to the faith of Israel was made. The international and national stability of these times constitute an important factor in establishing the total context of the prophet's ministry.

Social conditions during the reign of Jeroboam II were at the point of deterioration. "There was something rotten in the state of Israel in spite of the halcyon days it enjoyed under Jeroboam II," observed Wellhausen. "From the indirect results of war, from changes in the tenure and in the culture of the soil, from defective administration of justice, the humbler classes had much to suffer; they found that the times were evil."[8] One has but to read the messages of Amos, Hosea, Micah, and Isaiah to discern the validity of such an observation.

The prosperity that accompanied the era of peace introduced during the reign of Jeroboam II brought with it significant and far-reaching social changes in the life and thought of Israel. Primary among the social upheavals of the day was the development of an economic aristocracy and the first appearance of a class of defenseless poor. As the nation passed from an agricultural to a

---

[6] Clyde T. Francisco, *Introducing the Old Testament* (Nashville: Broadman Press, 1950), p. 254.

[7] *Ibid.*, p. 100. Amos' reference to the God of Israel as one "who makes morning darkness and treads on the heights of the earth" (4:13) associates both eclipse and earthquake, although not necessarily equating them chronologically.

[8] Julius Wellhausen, *Prolegomena to the History of Ancient Israel* (New York: Meridian Books, 1957), p. 470.

commercial society, all of the problems attendant upon the development of a large city and the urban community appeared. Government itself was corrupted and a rising tide of immorality was associated with the highly concentrated wealth of the day. For all practical purposes there was no "middle class" in Israel, their society being roughly divided into the "have" and the "have nots." [9]

Such significant changes in the social structures of the day called for new and forthright applications of the eternal element within the message of God. The effort of Amos, however, lay not in proclaiming a revolution in order to meet the changing social needs; rather, he proclaimed with fervor (cf. 5:1 ff.) the need for a reformation of heart and life along the lines of the covenant experience already laid down (cf. 3:1 ff.).

Morally, the land was suffering under the corruption produced as a by-product of Canaanite and Tyrian Baalism. In addition was the almost inevitable decay that is attendant upon misdirected prosperity. It was a rather strange anomaly that the very corruption of Israelite society could be traced, first, to current religious structures and, second, to the material prosperity which the ancient Hebrew interpreted as a sign of divine favor. Despite the contradictory nature of the circumstances, the debauched moral condition of the land was the product of both corrupted religion and perverted material prosperity. Rampant luxury and self-indulgence were manifest on every hand.

The dwellings of these men were of "hewn stone" (Am. v.11b), and some were ivory-fitted (iii.15). Not a few were built in the combination of "summer house" and "winter house" (iii.15). Though it would be a mistake to lay too much stress upon the use of a word, yet it is not without significance that the term which Amos employs to denote the dwellings of the upper class is "palace," or castle (Hebrew 'armon). In the houses were couches, often inlaid with "ivory" (vi.4a), and furnished with "damask" cushions (iii.12b). Food might be of choice "lambs," or of "calves of the stall" (vi.4b). Wine was drunk by the bowlful (vi.6a), the women being drinkers as much as their husbands (iv.1). With the choicest of oils the people anointed themselves (vi.6).[10]

---

[9] Roy L. Smith, *The Bible and the First World State* ("Know Your Bible Series" [New York: Abingdon-Cokesbury Press, 1943]), pp. 17-19.

[10] Richard S. Cripps, *A Critical and Exegetical Commentary on the Book of Amos* (2d ed.; London: SPCK, 1955), p. 6.

The nation was also guilty of the exploitation of the poor (cf. 2:6; 3:10; 4:1; 5:11; 8:4-6), and there was a lack of equitable justice in the land. A mechanical or magical relationship had been substituted for personal religion. The sin of arrogance and pride manifested itself in the popular idea that no evil could possibly come upon either the land or the people.[11] In the face of such degenerate morality, little wonder that the primary theme of Amos is expressed in his exhortation to "let justice roll down as waters, and righteousness as a mighty stream." [12]

The religious life of the era was little, if any, stronger than the social and moral fiber of the nation. Two threats plagued the religious structures of the day: the influence of Baalism with its insidious temptations, and the superficiality of normative Israelite religion.

Canaanite religion was closely linked with the cycles of nature. When the earth "died" following the blast of the summer heat and drought, it was felt that through the use of sympathetic magic the deities of fertility could be awakened or, in some instances, resurrected from the dead. This concept is suggestively reflected in the fact that the Hebrew word for death is identical with the name of a Canaanite god, Mot, who died each year with the summer drought.[13] Through this fertility cult, the Canaanite believed it possible to resurrect the dead god and bring life and fertility to both field and flock. Concerning this, Knight has given a good summary.

To human beings has been given the mysterious power of creating life. From the union of a man with a woman comes the procreation of a child. This basic, elementary, and yet vital aspect of human life was linked by the Canaanites with their worship of the spiritualized powers of nature. The physical union of men and women for procreative purposes the Canaanites integrated into their cult. With the form of a mighty, vital bull before their eyes, the veritable symbol of all procreative force, they sought to revive the life of nature at the end of the cycle of the year by encouraging "sacred prostitution" on the part of both men and women at the innumerable shrines of Astarte.[14]

[11] John Paterson, The Goodly Fellowship of the Prophets (New York: Charles Scribner's Sons, 1949), pp. 33-34.
[12] Francisco, op. cit., p. 101.
[13] George A. F. Knight, Hosea (London: SCM Press, 1960), p. 18.
[14] Ibid.

primarily a herdsman, he was also a "pincher of sycamores"—a reference, in all probability, to the hand pollination of the fruit tree. This process was well known in Mesopotamia and practiced to some extent in Palestine.[18] The very solitude of his task gave Amos time for reflection upon the needs of the land. However, he gave thought not only to the needs which existed, but also to the possibilities of a reformation of life and thought under God. This background was a basis for Amos' prophetic work.

It was in this same wilderness that Jesus was with the wild beasts during the forty days of his temptation. Here, too, John the Baptist was schooled for his ministry. David had been a shepherd in Bethlehem, a few miles away. Elijah, although across Jordan, was trained in this same background.[19] "Since Amos therefore was trained in the same school as so many of the finest, strongest, and most spiritual characters of his people," says Gwynn, "we are the less surprised at the high quality of his courage, physical, intellectual, moral and spiritual."[20]

Despite the isolation of his life as a shepherd, Amos was far from an uninformed provincialist. As Kuhl has pointed out, "From his acquaintance with geography, history (Amos mentions the names of 38 towns and districts), . . . legendary and proverbial wisdom (V.13, VI.12; cf. Amos's observations on 'cause and effect' in III.3 ff.), it is obvious that he was not an uneducated yokel."[21] He could speak of the Nile of Egypt (9:5b) and possibly the Euphrates ("the river" in Hebrew, 9:5a). He knew of the Nubians of Africa and the beginnings of both the Philistines and the Syrians, or Aramaeans.

These, and other obvious examples, underscore the fact that the prophet was well acquainted with the world of his day. W. Robertson Smith has pointed out: "It is obviously illegitimate to ascribe this fulness of knowledge to special revelation; Amos, we may justly conclude, was an observer of social and political life before he was

---

[18] Walter G. Williams, *The Prophets: Pioneers to Christianity* (New York: Abingdon Press, 1956), pp. 151 f.

[19] R. M. Gwynn (ed.), *The Book of Amos* (Cambridge: At the University Press, 1927), p. xi.

[20] *Ibid.*

[21] Curt Kuhl, *The Prophets of Israel*, trans. Rudolf J. Ehrlich and J. P. Smith (Edinburgh: Oliver & Boyd, 1960), p. 59.

a prophet, and his prophetic calling gave scope and use to his natural acquirements." [22]

Amos had a keen awareness of history and appealed to it as the arena of God's judgmental and redemptive activity for Israel. He knew the account of Jacob and Esau (1:11), spoke of the forty years wandering in the wilderness, and was aware of the gigantic stature of the Amorites (2:9-10). The fate of Calneh and Hamath were known by him, and the origin of both the Philistines and the Syrians was considered as common knowledge.[23] He recognized the element of purposiveness in history. In fact, "the teleological element, instead of being absent from his book, permeates the whole of it . . . he had a very definite conviction with reference to the ultimate triumph of the kingdom of God . . . it was this conviction that made him bold enough to announce with such fidelity his message of doom." [24]

As an observer of contemporary Israelite life, Amos was a man of keen perception and discernment. George Adam Smith has said, "he knew a mirage when he saw one." [25] He had the rare ability to see the facts, appraise the situation, and then act under the leadership of God to meet the particular issue at hand. As Eiselen has observed, "Amos brought from the desert a penetrating vision, a quickened conscience, and keen powers of discernment." [26]

While he possessed this sense of perception, Amos also maintained a strong sense of objectivity. His home in Judah, so far removed from Israel, did not cause him the heartbreak of a Hosea. Neither did his personal involvement precipitate the traumatic experience of a Jeremiah. He was relatively "free alike from the drugging influence of familiarity and from the numbing sense of inevitable complicity in the evils which he so clearly sees." [27]

[22] *The Prophets of Israel and Their Place in History* (2d ed.; London: Adam & Charles Black, 1902), p. 128.

[23] A. F. Kirkpatrick, *The Doctrine of the Prophets* (3d ed.; London: Macmillan & Co., 1917), pp. 104 ff.

[24] Knudson, *op. cit.*, pp. 87 f.

[25] *The Book of the Twelve Prophets* (rev. ed.; Garden City: Doubleday, Doran & Co., 1929), I, 83.

[26] F. C. Eiselen, *Prophecy and the Prophets* (New York: The Methodist Book Concern, 1909), pp. 40 f.

[27] W. O. E. Oesterley and T. H. Robinson, *An Introduction to the Books of the Old Testament* ("Living Age Books" [New York: Meridian Books, 1934]), p. 367.

This objectivity produced a detachment that gave Amos a certain note of austerity. Yet, while one does not find in Amos the personal involvement of many prophets, his objectivity should not be understood to be a lack of concern for Israel. Many have portrayed Hosea and Amos as opposites; Hosea stressing the love of God, and Amos emphasizing the justice of God. While these categories may be applied in a general fashion, they should not be allowed to obliterate the fact that Amos was quite concerned for the welfare of Israel (cf. 7:1-9). He loved Israel as few men have realized; but without his sense of objectivity, Amos could never have been a proper vessel to have been used in the proclamation of judgment upon the sins of Israel.

The objectivity of Amos gave him a forthrightness of presentation desperately needed in his generation. He called sin by its various names. No one went away wondering what was involved in the prophet's understanding of "sin." Sutcliffe has pointed out: "Again and again it happens that people blind themselves to their faults and make soothing excuses for their wrong-doing. And when pleasant persuasion fails, they need someone to come and speak plainly, even harshly, and with all the emphasis he can, to make them see." [28]

In the proclamation of his message the prophet was a literary master and an incomparable preacher. Driver quotes W. Robertson Smith concerning Amos' literary ability:

The language, the images, the grouping are alike admirable; and the simplicity of the diction, obscured only in one or two passages by the fault of transcribers, is a token, not of rusticity, but of perfect mastery over a language, which, though unfit for the expression of abstract ideas, is unsurpassed as a vehicle for impassioned speech. To associate inferior culture with the simplicity and poverty of pastoral life is totally to mistake the conditions of Eastern society. [29]

As a preacher, Amos constructed no two of his addresses along the same lines. Variety of expression constituted a strong element in his power. Although he had never heard the term "psychology," he knew the working of the human mind. "He so controlled the

---

[28] T. H. Sutcliffe, *The Book of Amos* (London: SPCK, 1939), p. 27.
[29] S. R. Driver, *The Books of Joel and Amos* ("The Cambridge Bible" [Cambridge: University Press, 1915]), pp. 103-4.

mental reactions of those who were his audiences," says Wolfe, "that even his opponents were temporarily helpless before him." [30] An examination of his style reveals:

Irony, sarcasm, playing on the prejudices of his audiences, the strategy of surprise, and numerous other devices were restored to on appropriate occasions but were never overused. In the ability to employ these marginal techniques sparingly but wisely, he was following in the footsteps of the greatest of his predecessors, Micaiah ben Imlah.[31]

In all that the prophet did, he was a rebel, a nonconformist. However, Amos was not a rebel for the sheer novelty of the experience or for the sake of being obstinate. Rather, the prophet perceived that the way of God was a path quite divergent from the way of Israel. He could do nothing other than rebel against the strictures of Israelite religion since this was necessary in order to follow the purposes of God as he understood them. "He functioned as a prophet was expected to do," says Williams, "but he refused to be labeled as one, . . . he was the kind of individual who has been responsible for putting conscience into religion." [32]

In his encounter with God, Amos plumbed the very depths of the divine communion available to man. His faith was characterized by a stark realism that could face with courage the irreligious elements of surrounding cultures, the superficiality of accepted religion, or the institutionalism of a corrupt priesthood. Life with God, as seen in Amos, confronts one with the startling realization that here is a religious experience for the market place and for the rough-and-tumble of life, as well as for the seclusion of the temple. The evaluation given of Artur Weiser's publication on Amos captures this aspect of the prophet's personality: "This work has earned deserved praise for its contribution to the study of prophetic religious experience and its insistence that the message and work of a prophet can only be understood when seen in the light of his 'experience with God.'" [33]

---

[30] R. E. Wolfe, *Meet Amos and Hosea, the Prophets of Israel* (New York: Harper & Bros., 1945), p. 63.

[31] *Ibid.*, pp. 62-63.

[32] *Op. cit.*, p. 151.

[33] John D. W. Watts, *Vision and Prophecy in Amos* (Grand Rapids: Wm. B. Eerdmans Publishing Co., 1958), p. 27.

The brevity of Amos' ministry, constituting "a mere episode in an obscure life," [34] underscores the tremendous impact that one life, surrendered to God, can make not only upon one's own generation, but upon the destiny of civilization itself. Amos never knew the vocation of an Isaiah who labored for many years after his divine call. His was not a response in youth to serve for a lifetime as in the case of Jeremiah. As W. Robertson Smith has stated: "Amos is a man of one prophecy. Once for all he had heard the thunder of Jehovah's shout, and seen the fair land of Canaan wither before it." [35] To every prophet of every generation, the brevity of Amos' ministry emphasizes the fact that it is not so much the length of service, as it is what is done with the time that one has to utilize for God, that is of most significance in life.

Considering the total impact of the prophet's life as a man committed to God, one is impressed with the fact that "Amos . . . is one of the most wonderful appearances in the history of the human spirit." [36]

Amos: The Message

No attempt will be made at this point to deal exhaustively with the message of Amos. This will be done in the remainder of the book. However, in order to understand the method of treatment followed in the succeeding chapters, it will be necessary to indicate a number of presuppositions and general principles involved in the exegesis and interpretation of the book of Amos.

Structure of the book.—The compiler (both the introductory statement and the narrative portion in the third person would indicate the work of an editor who placed the material in its present form) arranged the material in the book according to three main divisions. Whether the materials utilized constitute the entirety of Amos' words is highly debatable. The book may contain all that he spoke, or the material may be only representative of

---

[34] W. R. Smith, *op. cit.*, p. 128. J. D. Smart has suggested that the ministry of Amos "may have been only a few months or even less." Cf. "Amos," *The Interpreter's Dictionary of the Bible* (New York: Abingdon Press, 1962), A-D, 118.

[35] *Ibid.*

[36] G. A. Smith, *op. cit.*, p. 71, citing Cornill, *Der Israelitische Prophetismus,* 1894.

the prophet's ministry (cf. John 21:25 for a comparable treatment of Jesus' testimony).

Chapters 1 and 2 constitute a unit beginning with a formula that was probably a traditional cultic introduction (cf. Joel 3:16; Jer. 25:30-31). This prescribed form is modeled on a pattern resembling the ritual behind the Egyptian Execration Texts. The entire section, 1:3 to 2:16, places a curse upon the world first and then upon Israel herself, attempting in this to purge the world and the people.[37]

The second major division is found in chapters 3 through 6 and may be variously subdivided. The phrase "Hear this word . . ." introduces three subdivisions: 3:1-15; 4:1-13; and 5-6. There is an emphasis in each of these sections upon the manner in which the covenantal responsibilities have been violated through immoral conduct and superficial religion. Another alternative is to take chapters 3 through 6 as a section made up of lesser divisions introduced by both "Hear this word . . ." (3:1-15; 4:1-13; 5:1-17) and "Woe to . . ." (5:18-27; 6:1-14). This method avoids undue length in the latter subdivisions and will be followed in the present treatment of Amos. However the section may be subdivided, the division obviously extends from chapter 3 through chapter 6 and condemns both moral and religious infidelity.

The final division extends from chapter 7 through chapter 9. It contains a series of five visions (7:13; 7:4-6; 7:7-9; 8:1-14; 9:1-8) interrupted by a historical interlude (7:10-17). At the conclusion of the fifth vision, there is an epilogue promising the restoration of prosperity to the land (9:8b-15).

Unity of authorship.—The treatment of any prophet demands that honest consideration be given to the problem of authorship. Is the acknowledged author responsible for the entire work, or are there later additions which have been made to the book? The introduction of this book, phrased in the third person, is obviously from another hand, as is the historical interlude found in chapter 7. The problem of authorship runs much deeper than such superficial matters as the introduction and the narrative section, however, and must be considered with realism. The present treatment of Amos is not intended to be concerned primarily with

---

[37] Aage Bentzen, *Introduction to the Old Testament* (Copenhagen: G. E. C. Gad Publisher, 1949), II, 140.

the matters of unity and authorship. But at least some indication must be made concerning the assumptions made with regard to the more questionable passages in the book. Space does not permit a detailed presentation of the evidence. For the interested reader a number of excellent introductions and commentaries are available to present the evidence in each instance.[38]

Various areas within the book of Amos have been questioned concerning unity of authorship. These include scribal annotations and editorial additions (1:1; 4:7,12,13; 5:25-27), historical allusions inconsistent with the age of Amos (1:9-12; 5:1,2; 6:2,14; 8:11-13, etc.), references to Judah, theological ideas of a later age (2:4,5; 6:1), and the promises of hope and deliverance found in the book.[39] The wide range of opinion present concerning this issue is apparent in the fact that G. A. Smith, on the one hand, insists that only 26 or 27 verses out of 146 can be validly challenged; while R. E. Wolfe insists, on the other hand, that at least one half of the book as it now stands does not belong to Amos.[40] Note that the trend among more recent introductions and special studies is to recognize more authentic material than in earlier days of Old Testament scholarship. For example, H. H. Rowley indicates that "the genuineness of a few passages has been questioned. These include the oracle against Judah in ii. 4 f., and the concluding verses of the book, ix. 8b-15." [41] Both Gottwald and Bentzen have indicated that it is not possible to declare all promises of future hope postexilic on the basis that the prophet could not have anticipated such a time of bliss, since he was a prophet of "doom." [42]

The most important of the passages which have been questioned is 9:8b-15. Strong evidence has been presented for later authorship, as is summarized in the following:

[38] G. W. Anderson, A Critical Introduction to the Old Testament (London: Gerald Duckworth & Co., 1959); Bentzen, op. cit.; Cripps, op. cit.; R. H. Pfeiffer, Introduction to the Old Testament (rev. ed.; New York: Harper & Bros., 1948).

[39] Raymond Calkins, The Modern Message of the Minor Prophets (New York: Harper & Bros., 1947), p. 19.

[40] Ibid., p. 18.

[41] The Growth of the Old Testament (London: Hutchinson's University Library, 1950), p. 111.

[42] Norman K. Gottwald, Studies in the Book of Lamentations (London: SCM Press, 1954), p. 90; Bentzen, op. cit., p. 142.

1. The many linguistic affinities between it and the works of exilic and post-exilic times. . . .

2. The fact that this picture of restoration is inconsistent with Amos's repeated announcements of entire destruction. . . .

3. A favorable attitude towards Judah, as distinct from Israel, is not characteristic of Amos.

4. The emphasis laid upon material blessings, extension of territory, etc., to the exclusion of every moral characteristic, is inconsistent with the attitude of Amos, whose whole message is ethical.

5. The fact that the passage contains echoes of later writings. . . .

6. The abruptness of transition from the announcement of destruction to the promise of restoration. . . .

7. The use of the title ['lhyk] is in opposition to the usage and thought of Amos.

8. Amos always represents the whole people as the object of punishment, but here a distinction is made between the righteous and the sinner which is characteristic of later thought.

9. The passage seems to look back upon a ruined nation. . . .

10. Amos always contemplates an exile in Assyria, not a scattering among the nations as here.[43]

Scholarship is about equally divided concerning the authorship of 9:8b-15. Many responsible modern scholars have upheld its authenticity;[44] while equally reputable men have indicated that the passage is a later addition, dating in all probability at least as late as the Babylonian Exile.[45] One must be careful, however, lest one's decision be based upon the personal appeal made by one or the other of the groups of contending scholars. At least two principles should guide in arriving at a conclusion. First, there is nothing intrinsically impossible in assuming the authenticity of the section. It is now generally accepted that the prophets cannot be categorically divided into prophets of "weal" and "woe," with a prophet of "woe" never giving a message of hope.[46] Second, to deny that Amos wrote the passage does not deny the validity of

[43] Harper, *op. cit.*, pp. 195-96.

[44] Cripps, *op. cit.*, p. 77, cites the following: von Orelli (1888), Mitchell (1893), Driver (1897), Valeton (1898), von Hoonacker (1908), Hans Schmidt (1917), Kohler (1917), Ed. Meyer (1906), Sellin (1922), Konig (1924), Meinbold (1903).

[45] *Ibid.*, pp. 76-77, cites Wellhausen (1892), G. A. Smith (1896), Nowach (1897), Marti (1904), Harper (1905), Duhm (1911), Riessler (1911), Gressman (1921), Cornill (1912), Weiser (1961), Anderson (1959), Kuhl (1961), Fosbroke (1956).

[46] Gottwald, *op. cit.*

the message. It still represents the revelation of God, despite the fact that it may not have come through Amos.

The view adopted herein is that 9:8b-15 is a later addition to the book of Amos. Among the more cogent reasons for this are: (1) To depict the future in such strongly physical terms as 9:8b-15 seems counter to the entire emphasis of Amos against the exaltation of the externalities of religion, and (2) 9:8b-15 presupposes the ruin of the city of David. Such a time of absolute devastation came only during the Babylonian era. Yet, the nature of the evidence forbids dogmatism at this point, and recognition must be expressed of divergent points of view. Since the passage does represent the hope of Israel and the revelation of God concerning the restoration of the land, it will be treated as an integral part of the message of the book. Concerning the matter of scribal emendations (e.g., the Judah passages), although admittedly later than Amos, they will be treated as a part of the book of Amos. However, they may well have come from Amos' disciples rather than from the prophet himself.

Continuing relevancy of the message.—No word is ever God's last word. Indeed, "The word of God never comes to an end. For this reason, prophetic predictions are seldom final. No word is God's final word." [47]

In order to ascertain the true nature and character of that word, however, one must stand at the vantage point of the original composition. It is simply impossible to hear correctly and fully the word of God in Scripture apart from an understanding of the total background of the passage. This, of necessity, involves the utilization of the positive contributions of literary and textual studies, the historical context of the passage, light shed by archaeological discoveries and interpretations, and all other efforts to reconstruct, as nearly as possible, the life situation of the prophetic message. In essence, the historical-critical procedure constitutes a primary tool for the biblical exegete.

However, there still remains a sense in which the "message" is not the message of Amos. It is the message of God for every man of every generation, the word of God breaking forth ever and ever

---

[47] Abraham J. Heschel, *The Prophets of Israel* (New York: Harper & Row, 1962), p. 194.

again to speak to the heart of man. It is an indictment, not of an ancient people alone, but of life in the twentieth century—or in the twenty-fifth century, should the world as it is now known remain until that time. The message is not one just for the then, but for the now; not a past, but a present tense must pervade it in its entirety. To capture its truth one must not attempt to reconstruct the times of the prophet, then laboriously transport one's self and one's congregation back twenty-seven-hundred years. Rather, the message must be seen as vitally alive and addressed to every man of every generation. Only as such existential participation character-izes both exegesis and preaching will the Lion still roar (1:2; 3:8). The prophet of eighth-century Israel confronts twentieth-century prophets to say, "the Lion hath roared." Today's teacher and preacher must capture this note of contemporaneity.

2

When the Circle Is Complete

Amos 1:1 to 2:5

The preaching of Amos set a pattern of argumentation which could well be followed by prophets of every age. As Blackwood has observed, Amos "began with a psychological approach that would serve as a model for any diplomat today." [1] A controversy or discussion should begin from a point of common agreement, an issue to which the answer or outcome will be agreed upon by both participants. Having thus established a basis of common agreement, the next step is to proceed to a questionable proposition; yet one upon which there will be inevitable agreement. Finally, one should move to the real point of argumentation, which cannot be denied in view of the acceptance of the two previous conclusions.

In a series of concentric circles, Amos denounced the rebellion which had taken place against Yahweh.[2] Beginning with a great encircling movement that included Damascus, Gaza, Tyre, Edom, Ammon, and Moab; he identified the rebellion with those outside the boundary of God's special revelatory process (1:2 to 2:3). Shrinking to a smaller circle, a similar rebellion was placed squarely upon the shoulders of Judah (2:4-5). Then coming to the crux of the issue, he pierced the heart of Israel with the startling denunciation: "For three rebellions of Israel, and for four, I will not turn it away" (2:6).

Everyone within the sound of Amos' voice would have agreed

---

[1] Andrew W. Blackwood, *Preaching from Prophetic Books* (New York: Abingdon-Cokesbury Press, 1951), p. 28.

[2] The name "Yahweh" has been used as the personal name for the covenant God of Israel, rather than "Jehovah" or "Lord," which follows widely-accepted practice.

19

with the proposition that the foreign nations should fall under the heavy hand of God's judgment. Questionable assent would also have been given to the assertion that the inhabitants of Judah would be encompassed by this judgment. Then, having won agreement thus far, Amos moved immediately to thrust into the very heart of the issue. If it was true that the nations outside the realm of God's special revelation were accountable, if Judah was to render account for the breadth of her sins; then it logically followed that Israel could not escape either. Israel, having given assent to the two basic presuppositions, could not deny the validity of the third. She, too, would be judged for the enormity of her sin.

Sin Against Conscience, 1:3 to 2:3

These nations had experienced even as Israel, although in modified form, both an exodus and a covenant. For such freedom from bondage as the nations achieved, they

also were granted by Yahweh [Amos 9:7-8], and with the Exodus from bondage they accepted, as did Israel, the law of Yahweh, though in the restricted form of a commandment to recognize the fellow-humanity among themselves in their conduct.[3]

In view of both the creative activity and the providential care of God over all men, there is an "exodus" experience for all. By virtue of the presence of a universal conscience, there is a "covenant" under which all men are responsible before God. Although the nations did not enter into covenant relationship in the same sense as did Israel, they were nonetheless responsible before God. As Brunner declares, "there is no human existence without a relation to God."[4]

A common conscience inherent in society.—All men everywhere are accountable to God, for all have to some degree an awareness of the requirements of God. They are responsible for the common, everyday activities carried out within the context of relationships that have a national and an international character. It should be

[3] Eric Voegelin, *Israel and Revelation* ("Order and History Series," Vol. I [Baton Rouge: Louisiana State University Press, 1956]), p. 470.

[4] Emil Brunner, *The Letter to the Romans* (Philadelphia: The Westminster Press, 1959), p. 17.

obvious that this is true or else there would have been no moral basis on which Amos could have condemned the nations.

Universal responsibility and accountability before God should occasion no greater surprise on the part of the interpreter than does the emphasis of Amos upon universal origins, clearly enunciated in 9:7. Universal responsibility is but the corollary of universal origins. It is understandable that God should set forth some basis of accountability which would lift all men above the level of sheer animal existence. The realm of true personality inevitably involves moral perception and responsibility.

The only alternative to this is a conception of God as one who brought about the rise of nations, but then left the people without counsel or insight. Thus, God would be condemning them to life on the narrow frontier between sheer existence and true life, between brute instinct and human personality, between "being" and "nonbeing." Such an attitude would not only represent the height of irresponsibility on the part of one's understanding of God, but would run headlong into the incontrovertible fact that men did possess some sense of common accountability concerning moral action. For evidence of this note the high moral consciousness in texts of the ancient Near East.[5]

The very nature of Amos' condemnation implied a common conscience. In six separate instances (1:3,6,9,11,13; 2:1) Amos used the word *pesha‘* (rebellion) to characterize the action of the foreign nations. The word *pesha‘* is often used to indicate an actual rebellion as in 1 Kings 12:19, "So Israel has been in rebellion against the house of David to this day." Such usage in Amos 1:2 to 2:3 presupposed the responsibility of all men, for one could hardly have rebelled against a nonexistent standard of morality.

Amos contended quite strongly that all men are responsible before God because of a common conscience which is inherent in the world through the action of God. With his emphasis upon ethical monotheism the prophet could do no less, for "if there is one God—there must be one standard of goodness and justice which he wished to see established throughout the whole world." [6]

---

[5] Cf. James B. Pritchard (ed.), *Ancient Near Eastern Texts Relating to the Old Testament* (Princeton: Princeton University Press, 1950).

[6] C. A. Alington, *A New Approach to the Old Testament* (London: G. Bell & Sons, 1937), p. 44.

Conscience compromised and violated.—The words of the prophet move back and forth with the rapidity of a weaver's shuttle as he portrays the ways in which the nations had compromised and violated this common conscience. It was not the deed alone which Amos condemned, however, but the principle which gave birth to the deed. In retrospect the contemporary exegete must look for the source, not for the specific, historical application alone, or the continuing message of the prophet's work will be silenced. Amos condemned specific evil deeds, to be sure, but he did so on the basis of principles that were much broader and far deeper than the specific indictments. In each statement there can be discerned a valid principle which is applicable to every generation. This is the continuing voice of God to every remnant of society.

Cruelty, reflecting inhumanity of feelings, characterized Damascus (1:3-5). With caustic words of indictment the prophet could say, "Thus said Yahweh: 'On account of three rebellions of Damascus, and on account of four, I will not begin to cause it to return on account of their threshing the Gileadite with threshing sledges of iron'" (1:3).

The threshing instruments of iron mentioned by the prophet refer, in all probability, to the planks studded with flint and iron which were pulled rapidly across the grain in the process of threshing.[7] However, examples of such usage as a method of punishment or torture are limited, if not nonexistent. Amos is best understood here in a metaphorical sense. The cruelty and inhumanity manifested by the powers of Damascus upon the Gileadites were so severe that they were compared to a literal threshing of Gilead with instruments of iron.

Whether it be the wanton cruelty of an invading army under an ancient and ruthless king, or the inhumanity of feelings reflected in modern society; God sees as clearly and discerns as precisely the inhumanity reflected. Whether it be men crushed under the threshing sledges of Amos' day, or struggling men crushed beneath the cruelty of a social structure which denies the worth of every individual; God still comes in judgment upon those who express in word or deed attitudes reflecting a basic inhumanity of

---

[7] E. A. Edghill, *The Book of Amos* (2d. ed.; London: Methuen & Co., 1914), p. 6.

feeling. Cruelty in any of its varied forms remains reprehensible, regardless of the generation in which it occurs.

Contempt for human personality was manifested by Gaza's treatment of peaceful villages (1:6-8). "Thus said Yahweh: 'On account of three rebellions of Gaza, and upon four, I will not begin to cause it to return because of their carrying into exile a complete captivity for the purpose of delivering (them) to Edom'" (1:6).

The modern conscience, accustomed to the Christian gospel and hundreds of years of social advance, may well see in the indictment of the prophet a denunciation of slavery as an institution. Yet, Amos, as did the people, no doubt accepted this institution as a part of the social structure of the day. What the prophet did condemn, and quite vehemently, was the carrying away of a whole captivity. The phrase "whole captivity" depends for its interpretation upon the understanding of the word $sh^el\bar{e}m\bar{a}h$ or "whole." The word itself is an adjective which is translated variously as "complete," "safe," or "at peace." It comes from a root word sh-l-m which means "to be complete." [8] The phrase under consideration may be translated "a peaceful captivity." Complete villages seemingly had been depopulated in order that slaves might be sold by the Philistines to the Edomites. "Amos is not attacking the ordinary custom of enslaving or selling prisoners of war," says Gwynn, "but denouncing an organized slave-raiding traffic of which Gaza was the emporium, much as Zanzibar served the slave-gang traffic denounced by Livingstone which carried off wholesale peaceful African tribes." [9] The analogy between the activity of Gaza and the offenses of the eighteenth and nineteenth centuries in the United States is so clear as to need no elaboration.

Back of this practice denounced by the prophet lay a basic contempt for human personality. No man with a reverence for human personality could carry away a complete village to be sold into captivity. No man with a sense of respect for the inherent feelings of the individual could deal in the slave traffic. This twofold violation of the conscience could take place only by men with a lack of respect for human life.

---

[8] The Old Testament concept of peace is based upon wholeness or completeness. The individual is at peace who is "whole" or "complete." The same is true of nations.

[9] *Op. cit.,* p. 4.

Even today, disrespect for human personality takes many forms which are never suspected. Yet, so long as men, created in the image of God, are denied the basic rights of freedom in a democratic society, human beings are held in contempt. It may be the struggling masses of minority racial groups that strive for self-realization and true freedom in a world that theoretically exalts freedom. It may be the conglomerate citizenry of the nation as a whole that has lost all value as individuals made in the image of God. The principle, nevertheless, is the same. God still comes in judgment upon those who violate the common conscience of mankind by their contempt for human personality.

Covenant breaking, reflecting infidelity, characterized the people of Tyre (1:9-10). Amos condemned this, saying: "Thus said Yahweh: 'On account of three rebellions of Tyre, and upon four, I will not begin to turn it away, on account of their delivering a complete captivity to Edom, and they did not remember a covenant of brothers'" (1:9).

By the time of Ezekiel, Tyre had become notorious for her traffic in slaves (Ezek. 27:13). Many feel that Tyre purchased slaves from the Philistines, of whom Gaza was representative, and then resold them to the Edomites and others.[10]

It was for another violation of the conscience, however, that Amos called Tyre into account. She had broken the "covenant of brotherhood," and in this had reflected a sense of infidelity in her dealings with her fellow people. Some have thought that the "covenant of brotherhood" referred to the friendly covenant between Hiram and David (1 Kings 5:1). While such a covenant did exist, it is not likely that it survived the hostilities of the Baal-Yahweh controversy epitomized in the duel between Jezebel and Elijah. In view of this, the "covenant of brotherhood" probably existed with the Phoenician cities rather than with Israel. Quite likely, a neighboring Phoenician city had been the victim of an attack by a ruthless conqueror from whom Tyre made purchases of slaves, forgetting the "covenant of brotherhood" between herself and the enslaved city. If this hypothesis is correct, then the breadth of his teaching is greatly enlarged in scope, Amos becoming the champion of all men everywhere, not just of Israel.

---

[10] Harper, *op. cit.*, p. 25.

Casting off of pity reflected the continual, untempered nature of Edom's wrath (1:11-12).

> Thus said Yahweh:
> > "On account of three rebellions of Edom and for four,
> > > I will not begin to turn it away,
> > because of his pursuing his brother with the sword,
> > > he stifled his compassion,
> > and consequently his anger tore perpetually,
> > > his overflowing rage he preserved continually" (1:11).

The sin of Edom lay in the continual nature of his wrath. Of this Amos said, "his anger tore perpetually." The word translated "tore" is from *tāraph* (to tear, rend, pluck). The word is used of wild beasts in a literal sense (Gen. 37:33; 44:28) and also metaphorically with a wolf (Gen. 49:27), a lioness (Deut. 33:20), or a lion (Psalm 17:12) as subject. The verb is quite expressive of the true nature of anger within one's heart, for anger is a raging force that tears as do wild beasts. While not implicitly taught in the passage, it is quite significant that such anger eventually devours the man himself and not his enemy. Anger is, indeed, a wild beast that tears perpetually, just as a young lion tears the fresh-killed carcass on the jungle floor.

Coupled with this was the parallel observation on Edom's nature: "he kept his wrath for ever." The verb *shāmar* (kept) may be variously translated "keep," "watch," or "preserve." The word is used in Genesis 41:35 of grain that is to be stored up and kept, while in Proverbs 4:21 it is used of wise words and sayings which are to be remembered and not allowed to escape. Both of these usages picture ideally Edom's action. Unwilling to show pity, Edom added to this crime by "nursing" his anger—holding on to it and guarding it lest it be allowed to diminish.

Again, Amos drove home his point. There is a common conscience which should disparage such action. Yet, Edom had compromised and violated conscience by this threefold action, especially by the persistent guarding or nursing of anger.

Compassion for the helpless was ignored, reflecting Ammon's desire for material gain at the expense of human personality (1:13-15).

Thus says the Lord:
"For three transgressions of the Ammonites,
    and for four, I will not revoke the punishment;
because they have ripped up women with child in Gilead,
    that they might enlarge their border" (1:13).

The charge brought against Ammon was so reprehensible that, at first reading, one is prone to regard it as having nothing to say to any situation other than the immediate context in which it transpired. Such is not the case, however. Lack of compassion for the helpless plus accompanying greed at the expense of human personality are both issues with which every generation must come to grips.

In a time of war the Ammonites had obviously carried out the practice of "ripping up women with child." A similar deed was mentioned when Elisha said concerning Hazael, "I know the evil that you will do to the people of Israel; you will set on fire their fortresses, and you will slay their young men with the sword, and dash in pieces their little ones, and rip up their women with child" (2 Kings 8:12). Obviously, this was a systematic effort made on the part of an enemy to exterminate not only the present population, but to prevent the further growth of the people.

Men today may not be guilty of wholesale crimes so gruesome, in specific detail, as ripping up a woman with child. Yet, is not the principle behind this not still violated just as often? Is not compassion for the helpless ignored as often today as ever it was in the time of the eighth-century prophets? Do not men today "enlarge their borders" at the expense of human personality just as in the days of Hazael of Damascus and the Ammonite raiders? The specific application may change from time to time, but the basic principle never does!

Consideration for human feelings had been abandoned by Moab (2:1-3). The ancient crime of tomb molestation occupied the center of the prophet's thought in the denunciation of Moab. "Thus said Yahweh: 'On account of three rebellions of Moab, and upon four, I will not begin to turn it away, on account of his burning bones of king of Edom to the lime'" (2:1).

The Moabites had taken the body of the king of Edom, after some military victory, and burned it to lime. While the actual deed was reprehensible, the principle which it violated ran deeper than the act itself, for it concerned the complete abandonment of any consideration for human feelings. Vindictive hatred had been allowed to displace common consideration for human feelings. As a result, the body of the vanquished king had been burned in a frenzy of hatred.

Since it was felt that in some way the bones were vitally associated with life, the crime of Moab was worse in the day of Amos than today. Just as the blood was felt to be the seat of life, life was also thought to be associated in some manner with the bones. "The bones were regarded in primitive times as especially containing 'life' and so possessing magic life-giving power," said Snaith, and "to destroy a man's bones is definitely and finally to make an end of him (Jer. 8:1-3)." [11] In his denunciation of this crime, Amos defended the cause of the non-Israelite and denounced such an outrage against the common conscience. "In this sense of the universality of the moral law and God's interest in all mankind," says Gwynn, "the humble shepherd is far in advance of his age." [12]

While men may no longer burn the bones of another in vindictive hatred, and tomb desecration is, by and large, a problem which does not demand personal involvement; the same cannot be said of the abandonment of any consideration for human feelings. Any time human feelings are ignored and the individual lightly dismissed as of inconsequential value, man is once again as guilty as were the Moabites of Amos' day. The principle which was violated in the burning of the king's bones exists even today. Consideration for human feelings should never be given up.

With the infinite care of a master builder, Amos thus reconstructed the diverse ways in which nation after nation had compromised and violated the common conscience which they possessed. Like the prosecutor of the modern courtroom, he brought indictment after indictment. To these he submitted his evidence, incontrovertible and undeniable in its validity. From the northeast to the southwest, from the northwest to the southeast, each of the six nations considered was shown to have violated this common conscience.

---

[11] Norman H. Snaith, *Amos, Hosea and Micah* ("Epworth Preacher's Commentaries" [London: The Epworth Press, 1956]), p. 17.
[12] *Op. cit.*, p. 8.

The certain condemnation of those abandoning the dictates of a common conscience.—In the face of blatant disregard for the universal conscience inhering in the heart of every nation, each succeeding group was declared to have been under the judgment of God. Amos' picture of all nations as people with judgmental responsibility before God represented a surge of theological emphasis that went far beyond his own day. Damascus, Gaza, Tyre, Edom, Ammon, and Moab alike were described as being under the judgment of God for the conduct delineated in Amos 1:3 to 2:3.

The cumulative nature of the sin upon which judgment came was depicted clearly by Amos. The particular sin isolated in each case by the prophet represented neither the first nor the only type of violation by the nations. In each instance the prophet began his oracle, "For three transgressions (rebellions) . . . and for four." The rabbis and others of equally literal disposition saw in this expression the statement that while three transgressions will be forgiven, that God will come in judgment upon the fourth.[13] Such an interpretation misses the spirit of the entire passage, however, and the phrase should be taken as a literary device whereby the prophet indicated the accumulative nature of the nation's sin. Edghill observes, "Other numbers are often employed in scripture with the same sense: thus one and two Ps. lxii.11; two and three Amos iv.8, Hosea vi.2, Isa. xvii.6; four and five Isa. xvii.6; five and six 2 K. xiii.19; six and seven Prov. vi.16; seven and eight Mic. v.5." [14] The accumulative and indefinite number of each nation's transgressions are, therefore, marked out with clarity. The judgment of God came only after long patience and did not expend its wrath upon the first wayward step taken in rebellion. The sin specified in each case was only indicative of a larger number. It was a single example of numerous rebellions.

The consequences of sin are inevitable, underscored the prophet in his statement to each of the nations. To each succeeding group he said, "For three transgressions . . . and for four, I will not cause it to return." The Revised Standard Version translates this, "I will not revoke the punishment." It should be noted, however, that the Hebrew text, supported by the Septuagint, reads *lō' 'ashivennū,* or

[13]Edghill, *op. cit.,* p. 4.

[14] *Ibid.*

translated literally, "I will not cause *it* to return." Since the nation would logically seem to be the antecedent of "it," the phrase may also be taken to mean: "I will not cause the nation to return." In other words, forces of moral retribution have been set into effect by Israel's sin, but God will not overpower that principle or the nation. He will, rather, let the principle of retribution run its course in history. God will not intervene on Israel's behalf. As one writer has observed:

The "it" may be some previous threat of Amos, but it is perhaps more in accordance with the prophet's manner to regard it as that mysterious something which inevitably follows in the trail of sin. The world, as Amos saw it, was a world of law, a world in which deeds carried consequences, and causes produced effects. Sin drags Something on: on It is coming, nearer and nearer, and "I will not turn it back."[15]

The inevitable consequences of rebellion come on as a specter in the night to overtake and to suppress the rebel against God. The haunting "it" of every man's sin is a reality to be recognized and an inevitability for which one must prepare. In view of Amos' strong emphasis, one should be aware that "sins involve consequences that cannot be ignored or placated. Only divine mercy can grant reprieve and Amos does not believe that Yahweh is any longer disposed to forestall nemesis." [16] Sin and rebellion set in process retributive forces—the "it" of Amos' denunciation—that cannot be avoided. With every rebellion, there is the accompanying, inevitable consequence.

Certainty of judgment was depicted as ingrained in the mind of God. In the phrase, "I will also break the bar of Damascus" (1:5), and the succeeding five statements introduced by the same "I will," there is to be found the certainty of judgment. Such emphatic emphasis upon judgment is more noticeable in the Hebrew than in the English translations because of the peculiar nature of the Hebrew verbal system.

Two kinds of action are indicated in the Hebrew verb—complete and incomplete. A perfect (completed action) may be used for an action which has not yet taken place but which is viewed as

---

[15] John Edgar McFadyen, *A Cry for Justice: A Study in Amos* ("The Short Course Series" [New York: Charles Scribner's Sons, 1912]), p. 7.

[16] Norman K. Gottwald, *A Light to the Nations: An Introduction to the Old Testament* (New York: Harper & Bros., 1959), p. 285.

so certain by the prophet that, by virtue of the action of God or the experience of the prophet, he speaks of it as having already occurred. This is known as a prophetic perfect, a perfect of experience, or a perfect of certainty—each being but one shade different from the other.

At this point in the text Amos used such a perfect (completed action) to describe what God was going to do in the coming time. The English versions translate this as a future, "I will." This is acceptable provided one understands that the Hebrew is more positive than the English phrase, "I will," would indicate. The literal translation of the Hebrew *shillachti* would more nearly be "I have sent," "I sent," or "I have already sent." [17] Judgment was so certain in the mind of God that when the prophet spoke of it he used a verb that indicated completed action. Despite the fact that the deed of judgment had not yet taken place historically, it had already been performed in the mind of God.

The character of God's judgment, without exception in Amos 1:3 to 2:3, took the form of national catastrophe(s) through historical processes. Damascus would have its bar broken—the bar of the city gate which gave it security and protection—the loss of which would inversely bring disaster and annihilation. To this destruction of the city was added the threat of national exile to the locale from which the people had originally migrated—Kir (1:5). In rapid succession the prophet emphasized that Gaza and the surrounding nations were to be destroyed, utilizing the figure of fire, which was the most dreaded accompaniment of war, to indicate the downfall of each group. To this threat was also added, in most instances, the fact that leadership—"him who holds the scepter" (1:5,8), "their king . . . and his princes" (1:15), "the ruler . . . its princes" (2:3) —would be destroyed.

The judgment of God is viewed far too often by many modern men as some cataclysmic inbreak of God into history, totally apart from human instrumentality. This is far from the view of Amos and other Old Testament prophets. For them, God acted in the processes of history. Isaiah could speak of the Assyrian as a rod in the hand of God (Isa. 10:5), and Habakkuk could present the

---

[17] "I have kindled a fire" (1:14) and "I have cut off the ruler" (2:3) complete the six uses of the perfect to express the certainty of judgment in 1:3 to 2:3.

Chaldeans as men used in judgment upon Israel (Hab. 1:5 ff.). The prophets saw the hand of God in the rise and fall of nations, interpreting their ravaging thrusts into Israel or other nations as expressions of God's judgment. To what degree every event of history can be seen as the outworking of God's pattern and purpose is questionable. Yet, it is beyond question that the prophets so interpreted, time and time again, the rise and ravaging conquests of one nation after another. The judgment of God was definitely felt to be a part of the processes of history.

For the prophets there was no concept of God as breaking into history; he was already in history. Judgment for them did not involve the suspension of "natural law." Nothing existed apart from God. The very laws of the universe were but the expression of his activity. Indeed, the Hebrew vocabulary did not even have a word for "nature." It could only speak of God, and God was never thought of as removed from the daily events of life.[18] Many today, including devout Christian people, conceive of God as one far removed from the life and world of men. Now and again this God comes back to work a "miracle," or to come in judgment; then he returns to his own realm. This is completely antagonistic to the biblical view of the nature of God as found in the Old Testament. The Old Testament, especially Amos, conceived of God as one actively engaged in everything that takes place in life and the world. So much was this the case that they saw the evidence of God's judgment in the destructive foray of marauding enemy troops. For Amos, the character or nature of judgment lay in the events of history.

Sin Against Law, 2:4-5

Having drawn a large circle which included the nations immediately surrounding Israel, Amos then drew a smaller, concentric circle which included Judah, the Southern Kingdom. "The thunder draws nearer home and falls on Judah, not for these wild excesses of the heathen, but for the neglect of the law," says Horton.[19]

---

[18] Herein is to be found the most satisfactory understanding of "miracle" in the Old Testament.

[19] R. F. Horton (ed.), *The Minor Prophets: Hosea, Joel, Amos, Obadiah, Jonah, and Micah* ("The Century Bible," ed. Walter F. Adeney [Edinburgh: T. & T. Clark and E. C. Jack, n.d.]), p. 13.

"Judah is judged by the higher law of God's revelation, which imposes greater responsibilities." [20]

Privileged to have known the law of God, and blessed with a succession of religious leaders to instruct and counsel in the application of that law, Judah stood in greater responsibility than those who had never shared the light of the law. Judah had not sinned against an inherent conscience alone, but against the light of God shed through his law.

Revocation of punishment is not possible for Judah, 2:4a.—With rapier-like thrusts Amos emphasized that God "will not revoke the punishment." He will not turn "it" away. Again the prophet underscored the fact that there is an inescapable series of consequences involved in every act of rebellion. The law of God cannot be ignored with impunity. The revelation of his will, once made, raises the recipient into greater heights of responsibility before God. Whether it be ancient Judah waiting expectantly before the stroke of God's judgment, or modern western civilization breathlessly awaiting the next impact of a changing social order—the principle is the same. God comes in judgment upon his own. They are not immune to judgment because they are his. Indeed, their judgment is greater because they are his; yet, being God's, choose to rebel against his law.

The revelation of law to Judah makes revocation of judgment impossible, 2:4b.—The crime of Judah lay in the fact that they had known the law of God and did not sin in ignorance. A prophet of Judah two centuries later captured the thought of the times when he said,

> Thus says the Lord:
> "Stand by the roads, and look,
>   and ask for the ancient paths,
> where the good way is; and walk in it,
>   and find rest for your souls.
> But they said, 'We will not walk in it.'
> I set watchmen over you, saying,
>   'Give heed to the sound of the trumpet!'
> But they said, 'We will not give heed'" (Jer. 6:16-17).

---

[20] Herbert L. Willett, *The Prophets of Israel* ("Bethany C. E. Reading Courses" [New York: Fleming H. Revell Co., 1899]), p. 47.

It was such an attitude as this that made the reversal of punishment an impossibility. The present attitude prevented a return to God; indeed there was not any thought of following his law.

Rejection of the law, 2:4c.—The law of God remained central in the denunciation of Judah by the prophet. Yet, much more is included in the term "law" than the average person is aware. H. Wheeler Robinson has observed:

The important word rendered *law* has a variety of meanings; it may denote teaching in a general sense (Isa. 1:10), technical instruction given by a priest (Jer. 18:18), a written code of law (Ex. 24:12; Deut. 1:5; Neh. 8:1), and "the Law" as the first part of the Hebrew canon (Psa. 119). Here it must mean religious and moral teaching given in Jehovah's name by priest or prophet.[21]

The term "law" embraced far more than just a code. It included the totality of all instruction given by authorized personnel, the total revelation of God which had been received. In rejecting this law, Amos emphasized that Judah had done at least three things. First, they had forsaken the law of God. "They have rejected the law of the Lord," says the prophet, and in this Judah took a negative attitude toward the law which had been given.

Second, they had failed to keep God's command; they "have not kept his statutes." While this is but a synonymous way of stating that they forsook the law, it is set forth from a slightly different perspective. The word translated "statutes" (*chōq*) definitely refers to something prescribed, coming from a root verb which means "to cut in," "inscribe," or "decree." It reflects the concept of "law" in the more restricted sense of a code than does the word earlier translated "law" (*tōrāh*). In this twofold emphasis, Amos summed up the rebellious attitude of Judah toward both codified law and the totality of instruction given to the people by religious personnel.

Finally, Amos indicated that Judah had followed falsehood: "their lies have led them astray, after which their fathers walked" (2:4). Whether before the mountain which Moses ascended to receive the law, or later at pagan sites of worship; the people of

[21] "Amos," *The Abingdon Bible Commentary*, eds. Frederick C. Eiselen, Edwin Lewis, David G. Downey (New York: The Abingdon Press, 1929), p. 778.

God had somehow succumbed to their own false ideas as over against the will of God as revealed through both general religious instruction and codified law. Amos bluntly spoke of these misconceptions as "lies." He did not bring into question the sincerity of the average man as he falsely worshiped, nor the way in which he was at times misled by religious personages. He simply branded as a lie that which so deceived the people as to lead them to forsake the way of God.

Retribution follows the rejection of God's law with inevitability, 2:5.—"So," said the prophet, "I will send a fire upon Judah, and it shall devour the strongholds of Jerusalem." The judgment once again was depicted in terms of fire which, with famine, was one of the most feared accompaniments of warfare. In thus utilizing the same figure of speech to describe both the judgment of the foreign nations and Judah, Amos underscored the equality of judgment. Retribution follows the rejection of God's law with inevitability. Whether the violation was from Judah or the nations surrounding is inconsequential.

3

Revelation and Response
Amos 2:6-16

Turning in artistic climax to the people before whom he stood, Amos came to the heart of God's message. If the nations without law and revelation were guilty because of having compromised a common conscience, if Judah stood condemned for having sinned against all instruction and revelation of God; surely, Israel could not plead exemption from the heavy hand of God's judgment. Without knowing it, the waiting crowd passed judgment upon itself. As Paul later emphasized, "Therefore you have no excuse, O man, whoever you are, when you judge another; for in passing judgment upon him you condemn yourself, because you, the judge, are doing the very same things" (Rom. 2:1). In giving assent to the indictment of the nations and the accusations against Judah, Israel had paved the way for her own condemnation.

With piercing eyes and hurtling words that rushed to their mark, the prophet addressed Israel with the severe charge of having rebelled against God's love. The prophetic indictment of sin as basically against God's love [1] is supported ably by Amos' oracle against Israel, in which the burden of his case rested upon Israel's rebellion against the revealed love of God. "Israel's sin is against light and against love," says Paterson.[2] It is, therefore, worse than the sins of either the nations or of Judah. Indeed,

Israel's sin is deeper and blacker than that of other nations. She had sinned not only against conscience, but against the manifest love of God

---

[1] John P. Milton, *Prophecy Interpreted* (Minneapolis: Augsburg Publishing House, 1960), p. 95.
[2] *Op. cit.*, p. 32.

and against the special revelations of His will. She had acted against her better knowledge, and she had turned a deaf ear and a stubborn heart to the message of her great preachers.[3]

Ingratitude, whether directed toward God or toward one's fellow-man, is both inexcusable and reprehensible. The ungrateful person, whether in the realm of the spirit or in the common events of daily life, remains not only unappreciated but rejected. To sin against conscience is pathetic since it involves the rejection of a known, higher way. To sin against law is inexcusable since it is the fruit of self-will and utter rebellion of spirit. But to sin against the love of the one who stands behind both law and conscience is debasing. It reveals an inner lack of appreciation and love by the individual.

Response to God's Love, 2:6-8,12

Men respond in many ways to the love of God. For some there is the loving response of an Isaiah, "Here I am! Send me" (Isa. 6:8), the "Speak, Lord, for thy servant hears" of a Samuel (1 Sam. 3:9). For others, there is the fearful response of an Adam, "I heard the sound of thee in the garden, and I was afraid (Gen. 3:10), the despicable conduct of Hophni and Phinehas, sons of Eli chosen to minister before God, but who were accounted to have been "worthless men; they had no regard for the Lord" (1 Sam. 2:12). A modern writer has observed that

> To every man there openeth
> A Way, and Ways, and a Way,
> And the High Soul climbs the High Way,
> And the Low Soul gropes the Low,
> And in between on the misty flats,
> The rest drift to and fro.
> But to every man there openeth
> A High Way and a Low,
> And every man decideth
> The Way his soul shall go.[4]

To Israel there did open two ways: the high way and the low way, the way of obedience and the way of rebellion, the way of

---

[3] McFadyen, op. cit., p. 16.
[4] John Oxenham, "The Ways," Gentlemen—The King (Boston: The Pilgrim Press). Used by permission.

respondent love and the way of ingratitude. Israel chose the low way. She responded to God's love by rejecting it.

Persecution of the helpless within the land, 2:6-7a.—

Thus says the Lord:
   "For three transgressions of Israel,
      and for four, I will not revoke the punishment;
   because they sell the righteous for silver,
      and the needy for a pair of shoes—
   they that trample the head of the poor into the dust of the earth,
      and turn aside the way of the afflicted."

The true measure of a man or a nation is to be observed in his treatment of those who, for one reason or another, are weaker and less powerful than he. It may be an inferior economic or social position; it may be in the area of intellectual attainment or in the realm of spiritual growth. The principle is the same. What a man is inevitably works itself out in such situations. Power and positions of influence may bring out the best in a man. On other occasions, they may bring out the worst. Yet, such situations only reveal what is already in a man. They do not necessarily stand as the contributory cause. This is to be found in the nature of his heart, in what he is. Israel manifested her true self in the persecution of the helpless within the land, striking in turn the righteous, the needy, the poor, and the afflicted.

Persecution by Israel took the form of judicial injustice, the weak man being unable to receive justice at the courts of law. The first denunciation, "they sell the righteous for silver," concerned the bribe which was so prevalent in the courts of eighth-century Israel. Not only Amos, but

all the great prophets bring a charge against the public administration of justice; see e.g. Isa. v. 23; Mic. iii. 9-11; Ezek. xxii. 29. The selling of justice is expressly alluded to in Isa. ix. 23, iii. 14. Deuteronomy, a document also proceeding from the prophetic school, attaches special value to civic justice, and enlarges upon the subject with considerable detail (e.g. Deut. xvi. 18-20).[5]

A second type of judicial injustice is manifested in the phrase, "and the needy for a pair of shoes." This has often been under-

---

[5] Cripps, *op. cit.*, p. 140.

stood to refer to the unscrupulous action of the rich as they oppressed the poor by selling these creditors into slavery for a trifling sum, the mere price of a pair of shoes. This understanding of the phrase is inadequate for at least two reasons. In the first place, the phrase, "the needy for a pair of shoes," is in synonymous parallelism with the phrase, "they sell the righteous for silver." In this case, the second member, which is questionable in meaning, should be interpreted in the light of the first parallel member, whose interpretation is quite clear. This represents a valid use of synonymous parallelism as an aid to interpretation. Second, if "the needy for a pair of shoes" be understood as referring to the oppression of the poor outside the courts; then verse 7, "they that trample the head of the poor into the dust of the earth," is redundant, if not useless in terms of an advance in the prophetic message.

"Selling the needy for a pair of shoes" does not have reference to the oppression of the poor outside the court, but refers directly to the oppression of the poor man in the courts of the day. The "pair of shoes" should be understood in light of the practice of exchanging a sandal when property was sold, the sandal becoming a sign or symbol of property rights involved. The practice of selling land by the transfer of a shoe was prevalent, according to Horton. He indicates that the practice is found in Ruth 4:7, Psalm 60:8, and that 1 Samuel 12:3 in the Septuagint reads, "of whose hand I received a bribe or a pair of shoes?" The shoe may, therefore, be regarded, he concludes, "as the title deed of the poor man's inheritance which the rich man appropriated." [6]

Such an understanding avoids the necessity of shifting from the unjust judge to the rapacious creditor in the same phrase. It leaves the way for the accusation in verse 7 to fall as a new charge of persecution of the poor outside the courts. Also, it meets the demands of synonymous parallelism—the second member expressing an idea identical with the first member, although in different words.

Persecution was not limited to the courts, however, and the rich were graphically portrayed as "they that trample the head of the poor into the dust of the earth" (2:7). The phrase is quite vivid when translated more literally, "the ones trampling upon the dust the head of the poor." The action of the rich was so vicious that

---

[6] *Op. cit.*, pp. 132 f.

Amos could describe it as crushing into the dust the very heads
of the poor. The word "trample" is identical with that found in
Genesis 3:15: "He shall bruise your head, and you shall bruise his
heel." [7] Seldom is there found so vivid a picture of persecution of
one group by another as at this point. The poor had literally had
their heads crushed into the dust of the earth by their rich
oppressors.

Finally, the persecution took the form of turning "aside the way,
of the afflicted" (1:7b). The helpless were accounted worthy of
every consideration in ancient Israel. There is every reason to
suppose that this concern was implemented by acts of kindness
toward the less fortunate. Job, in presenting a Hebrew ideal for
manhood, states:

> If I have withheld anything that the poor desired,
>   or have caused the eyes of the widow to fail,
> or have eaten my morsel alone,
>   and the fatherless has not eaten of it
>
> . . . .
>
> if I have seen any one perish for lack of clothing,
>   or a poor man without covering;
> if his loins have not blessed me,
>   and if he was not warmed with the fleece of my sheep;
> if I have raised my hand against the fatherless,
>   because I saw help in the gate;
> then let my shoulder blade fall from my shoulder,
>   and let my arm be broken from its socket.
> For I was in terror of calamity from God,
>   and I could not have faced his majesty (31:16-23).

In the face of such a high and noble idea as this, the action of
Israel in "turning aside the way of the afflicted" was even more
serious in its nature. Action of this nature revealed the true condition of Israel's heart. Placed in a position of power, Israel turned
aside the way of the afflicted.

---

[7] The RSV translation "trample" as opposed to "pant after" is based upon
an emendation of the Hebrew shā'aph (pant after) to shūph (trample). This
is based primarily upon the Septuagint—"the ones treading upon the dust of
the earth" (the Septuagint pateō being used as a means of translating the
Hebrew shūph). A translation of all of verse 7 in the Septuagint will reveal the
difficulty of the Septuagint translator with this verse.

Perversion of life as reflected in immoral actions, 2:7b-8.—To those as sensitive as were the prophets, the perversion of life produced by the immoralities associated with some forms of worship in Israel constituted a traumatic shock. Sacred prostitution had long been practiced by the Canaanites, and Israel had not dwelt long in the land until the ritual was introduced at Israelite shrines (cf. 1 Kings 15:12; Hos. 4:14). Beginning as part of a religion which gave primary emphasis to the fertility of the flock and the field, sacred prostitution had become an integral part of Canaanite worship. What began as dramatization of the love life of the gods, a drama enacted by the priests of the shrine and women devotees, "had now descended," says Williams, "to the place of being little else than a wholesale practice of lust and licentiousness. Amos labeled it for what it was, immorality and adultery." [8]

This was the sight which Amos depicted: "a man and his father go in to the same maiden, so that my holy name is profaned; they lay themselves down beside every altar upon garments taken in pledge" (2:7b-8a). In the face of this sensuality, which many in Israel accepted as commonplace, Amos' words thundered forth as the voice of doom upon such immorality returned for God's love.

Associated with the immorality already mentioned, were two accompanying deeds indicative of the depths to which Israel had fallen. The very garments upon which the acts of ritual prostitution were committed were garments taken in pledge. These were garments surrendered by the poor for the nonpayment of debt, but items which under Israelite law should have been returned to the owner each night (Ex. 22:26-27). "Nothing is more loathsome in the sight of man or God than immorality under the hypocritical guise of religion," states a modern writer.[9] Amos spoke his word concerning this almost twenty-seven-hundred years ago.

Not content with having pointed out this depravity, Amos continued by emphasizing that the very wine which they drank was "the wine of those who have been fined" (2:8b). The prophet had reference either to wine that had been collected as fines for some

[8] *Op. cit.,* p. 157.
[9] Charles Foster Kent and Robert Seneca Smith, *The Work and Teachings of the Earlier Prophets* (New York: Young Men's Christian Association Press, 1907), p. 13.

civil judgment, or to wine which had been collected as a fine levied through the priest. If the latter be the case, then the picture drawn by Amos was one in which the profanation of that which was holy added to the number of Israel's sins.

Although true to human nature, the picture which Amos portrayed was repulsive. Not only was individual life corrupted, but the total family life as well, for "a man and his father go in to the same maiden." There is no more vivid portrayal of degradation in all of the prophets than the one at this point. A man and his father went in to the same cult prostitute. There at the very altar of God, upon garments taken in pledge from the poor of the land, Israel deteriorated before God. With wine taken as fines, the revelry progressed as Israel added yet another rebellion against God.

In the face of the immoralities of every age, the true prophet of God should remember that

every sin has a name. God's prophet does not stop at expiating upon our human sinfulness. He does not only address us as men who "have despised the law of the Lord, and have not kept his commandments, and their lies caused them to err, after the which their fathers have walked." On the contrary, he goes on to specify sin in its utter obnoxiousness.[10]

As Luthi has observed, "My dear brethren in the ministry, and my dear fellow members of the Church up and down the country, we must ask God for the power to be able to speak more clearly about sin." [11] The true prophet of God sees sin for what it is. He calls it by its name without apology and having done this, he speaks fearlessly of the awful judgment of God upon it.

Prohibition of true religion, 2:12.—Often, the immediate response of people in a time of grossly sensual immorality is to attempt to stifle any voice of correction. Although there is no historical foundation for assuming a religious protest by either the Nazirite or the prophet, what is known of their office would indicate their automatic opposition. As a part of his vow, the Nazirite refused

---

[10] Walter Luthi, *In the Time of Earthquake,* trans. H. L. M. Haire and Ian Henderson (London: Hodder & Stoughton, 1940), p. 27.

[11] *Ibid.*

to partake of strong drink, and the very life of such a man stood as living judgment upon those who "in the house of their God . . . drink the wine of those who have been fined" (2:8b). In some manner Israel "made the Nazirite to drink wine." Having thus compromised himself, he ceased to be a symbol of protest. Such remains the case today when holy men can be led in one way or another to compromise themselves. Little does the world have to fear from the religious leader who has so compromised himself that he cannot speak out in judgment upon the sins of his society.

The prophet was more directly handled than was the Nazirite, for Israel "commanded the prophets, saying, 'You shall not prophesy'" (2:12). No men who have gone in as father and son to the same maiden want a prophet to speak of judgment. No group that has engaged in immorality at the altar of God upon garments taken in pledge from the poor of the land wants to hear a word of judgment. No man absorbed in the revelry produced by drinking wine taken in fines wants to hear the pessimistic note of a prophetic voice. Times have not greatly changed. In one way or another the modern prophet is still commanded, "You shall not prophesy!" The approach today may be more subtle, the methodology more acceptable, but the result is the same—voices that will not cry out in judgment as did the prophet from Tekoa.

Voices of protest were silenced. Holy lives which could have spoken more vocally than even the prophet's words were brought to an end. Indeed, the prohibition of true religion is the inevitable goal of a society set upon its own godless immoralities. Across a hundred generations or more, the effort in the presence of perverted lives has been to quiet voices of protest. Yet, to do this does not still the voice of God, for even when the Nazirite has been compromised and the prophet has been silenced, God still speaks. This is society's hope in every age.

In his denunciations against Israel, Amos made the manner in which she had responded to the love of God clear. The persecution of the helpless, the perversion of life through immoral actions, and the prohibition of true religion had been the collective response of Israel to God. In Amos' indictment, the crimes of a seemingly quiet village people were ranked as great, if not greater, than the ripping up of pregnant women by the Ammonites (1:13-15), or the slave trading of an ancient people (1:2-8). The sins of civilization are often even more cruel than the atrocities of barbarism. Men forget, says George Adam Smith, "that luxury, bribery, and intolerance, the oppression of the poor, the corruption of the innocent and the silencing of the prophet . . . are even more awful atrocities than the wanton horrors of barbarian warfare." [12] Twentieth-century sins of oppression in the areas of social injustice, economic maladjustments, and individual deterioration of character proceed out of the same alienation from God as that of which Amos spoke.

Revelation of God's Love: His Providential Care, 2:9-11

The failure of man does not mean the failure of God, however, and so long as God is God, his love will remain constant for the simple reason that "God is love" (1 John 4:8). That God loved Israel was a fact of experience and of history beyond denial. Not in just a single, isolated deed had this love been manifested, but through innumerable avenues of affection God had made known his love for the people. Of these numerous expressions of love and kindness Amos isolated three.

National origins due to his providence, 2:10a.—The fact that Israel existed as a nation was a manifestation of God's expressive love. "I brought you up out of Egypt," said Yahweh (2:10*a*), and in this decisive act of deliverance his love for helpless Israel was made plain. Amos had in mind Israel as the totality of north and south, for what he said could not have been said of one to the exclusion of the other. "It is arguable," says Gottwald,

that Israel in the oracle does not refer exclusively to the northern kingdom as a political entity but to the covenant people who embraced Hebrews in both kingdoms. The unity of north and south is more fundamental than the political breach. All the prophets appear to share the same conviction and to cherish the hope of reunion for the two peoples.[13]

Israel as a national entity was a miracle of God's grace and love. When the Deuteronomist considered Israel's insignificant stature as a slave people he was led to confess:

---

[12] *Op. cit.*, p. 120.
[13] *A Light to the Nations, op. cit.*, p. 285.

It was not because you were more in number than any other people
that the Lord set his love upon you and chose you, for you were the
fewest of all peoples; but it is because the Lord loves you, and is keeping the oath which he swore to your fathers, that the Lord has brought
you out with a mighty hand, and redeemed you from the house of
bondage, from the hand of Pharaoh king of Egypt (Deut. 7:7-8).

Nurture in days of growth provided by his protection, 2:9,10b.—
God did not bring Israel forth from Egypt to leave her stranded
upon the bare sands of history, without succor and without
strength.

> Yet I destroyed the Amorite before them,
>> whose height was like the height of the cedars,
>> and who was as strong as the oaks;
> I destroyed his fruit above,
>> and his roots beneath.
>
> . . . .
>
>> and led you forty years in the wilderness,
>> to possess the land of the Amorite,

spoke God through the prophet. No doubt existed in the mind of
Amos that God led not only in the forty years through the wilderness, but in the conquest and occupation which followed. Israel
was nurtured just as a child receives provision and sustenance from
its parents following birth. In this Amos anticipated the emphasis
to be made by the prophet Ezekiel, who keenly portrayed Jerusalem
saying:

And as for your birth, on the day you were born your navel string was
not cut, nor were you washed with water to cleanse you, nor rubbed
with salt, nor swathed with bands. No eye pitied you, to do any of
these things to you out of compassion for you; but you were cast out on
the open field, for you were abhorred, on the day that you were born
(16:4-5).

This could have been truly said of the entire nation. How dis-
tressingly accurate is this of the life of every man, apart from God:
"No eye pitied you, to do any of these things to you out of compassion for you; . . . for you were abhorred." (Ezek. 16:5). Yet,
miracle above all other miracles, God cared, God loved. For, continued the prophet Ezekiel:

When I passed by you, and saw you weltering in your blood, I said to you in your blood, "Live, and grow up like a plant of the field." And you grew up and became tall and arrived at full maidenhood; your breasts were formed, and your hair had grown; yet you were naked and bare. When I passed by you again and looked upon you, behold, you were at the age for love; and I spread my skirt over you, and covered your nakedness: yea, I plighted my troth to you and entered into a covenant with you, says the Lord God, and you became mine (16:6-8).

Was not the miracle of Israel's nurture and growth that God loved the unlovable? Is this not the confusing, yet moving splendor of every man's life? God could see the unloveliness and, yet, plight his troth and enter into covenant so that it could be said, "You became mine."

Needs of the spirit were met by his servants, 2:11.—"Man does not live by bread alone" (Deut. 8:3). In view of this basic precept God provided not only bread for Israel, but spiritual guidance as well. Nothing demonstrates so well the grace and love of God, whether in Israel or in the modern church, as the fact that God raises up "some of your sons for prophets, and some of your young men for Nazirites" (2:11). In terms of the counsel and the leadership they can offer in the quest to know God, such men reveal the love of God who made provision for such knowledge through their ministries. Also, in the fact that such men are normally called out of a godly and devoted background (cf. Samson, Judg. 13:2 ff.; 1 Sam. 1:3 ff.; and Jer. 1:1 ff.), love and commendation are both shown upon such devotion. The call of God is an expression of God's love and grace.

The prophet was the most outstanding religious personality of the Old Testament, although he would have been the first to have denied official religious connections because of the depths to which contemporary religious life had fallen (cf. 7:14). "Called, commanded, and commissioned, the prophet was summoned out of the world although he continued to live in it. He lived with God yet dwelt among men."[14] No higher tribute could have been paid to the prophet. Herein is the continuing challenge—to be at all times a man who lives with God, yet one who dwells among men.

---

[14] Otto J. Baab, *Prophetic Preaching: A New Approach.* (New York: Abingdon Press, 1958), p. 34.

The Nazirite, on the other hand, is a lesser known religious personality than the prophet. Everyone is acquainted with the prophet, but very few today are aware of the ministry of the Nazirite. Yet, his ministry was highly useful and contained many principles of lasting value. "Nazirite" is connected etymologically with the concept of consecration, as a brief citation of related words will reveal. The word *nāzîr*, translated "Nazarite," is literally "one consecrated, devoted." Closely related to this is another substantive, *nēzer*, meaning "consecration, crown, Naziriteship," the crown being a sign of one's consecration (cf. Gen. 49:26; Deut. 33:16; Lam. 4:7). Another substantive, *minzor*, is used for "princes," in that they are consecrated (i.e., anointed) ones.

The root verb *nāzar*, which stands behind both of the Hebrew substantives, is a denominative. Its meaning is derived from the substantives and, therefore, in terms of original meaning little can be gained from its study. In terms of usage, however, it is quite enlightening and is used variously as "to dedicate," "consecrate," "separate," as in the following:

For any one of the house of Israel, or of the strangers that sojourn in Israel, who *separates* himself from me, taking his idols into his heart and putting the stumbling block of his iniquity before his face, and yet comes to a prophet to inquire for himself of me, I the Lord will answer him myself (Ezek. 14:7).

Tell Aaron and his sons to keep away from the holy things of the people of Israel, which they *dedicate* to me, so that they may not profane my holy name (Lev. 22:2).

They came to Baal-peor, and *consecrated* themselves to Baal (Hosea 9:10).

Thus you shall keep the people of Israel *separate* from their uncleanness, lest they die in their uncleanness by defiling my tabernacle that is in their midst (Lev. 15:31).

The primary meaning of the term "Nazirite," according to lexicography, is that of "consecration." This was the primary concern of the Nazirite, and to that end he dedicated himself either for life or for a brief period of time. One could be consecrated to God prior to birth, as in the case of Samuel, although there is no evidence that he lived under this stricture in his actual ministry. Samson is also an example of a man used by God despite the lapse which characterized his life (Judg. 14-16). That an individual could consecrate himself as a Nazirite later in life and for a briefer perod of time is obvious from the instructions concerning the Nazirite (Num. 6:9-20).

The primary concern of the Nazirite was to manifest his consecration to God by a particular manner of life. This consisted of " (1) totally abstaining from products of the vine and all intoxicants —possibly an ancient Hebrew protest against the low ideals of Canaanite agriculturists; (2) refusing to cut their hair lest a man-made tool profane this god-given growth; (3) avoiding contact with the dead; and (4) declining unclean . . . food." [15] In these ways the Nazirite sought to express his devotion and dedication to God. This was his mode of life.

The Nazirite differed from the prophet in that the former attempted to impress Israel with the character of life which he lived to the exclusion of any other major emphasis. This is not to say that the prophet did not seek to uphold the highest ideals in his own personal life; it is simply to recognize a difference in the primary means utilized by each in the proclamation of the word of God.

The vocation of the Nazirite continues to exhibit a valid principle, although one would not approve every manifestation that his consecration took. The principle of seeking to live a life completely consecrated to God remains a worthwhile objective. The effort to demonstrate by deed more than by word, not only one's individual consecration but the message of God to one's society, is quite commendable. To this extent, the limited Nazirite vow should be assumed by every individual who is truly consecrated to God.

The fact that both prophet and Nazirite had been given to Israel cannot be denied. The indisputable nature of such an expression of God's love was manifested in the rhetorical question with which Amos concluded: "I raised up some of your sons for prophets, and some of your young men for Nazirites. Is it not indeed so, O people of Israel?"

---

[15] Madeleine S. and J. Lane Miller, *Harper's Bible Dictionary* (3d ed.; New York: Harper & Bros., 1952), p. 480.

Reaction of God to Israel's Response to His Revealed Love, 2:13-16

Stressing both the causative action of God and the inevitable fruit of such action, Amos depicted the response of God to the crimes of Israel. As the prophet had emphasized to each nation, "For three transgressions . . . and for four, I will not revoke the punishment."

Israel is to be put in her proper place by God, 2:13.—"Behold," said the prophet as he spoke for God, "I will press you down in your place, as a cart full of sheaves presses down." Accepting the Revised Standard Version translation, there can be no doubt about the picture in the mind of the prophet. Just as a cart full of sheaves presses down in agonizing weight, even so God is going to press Israel down in her place. Israel's place was not one of exaltation over against God. Her rightful position was subordinate to God, and it was to this position that she was to be pressed.

An alternate reading based on the Hebrew text is also possible for 2:13. It should be taken into serious consideration as possibly a more accurate translation than that of the RSV, although the RSV has the support of the American Standard Version in addition to the opinion of numerous modern scholars. It should be noted that the verb is definitely not the passive "I am pressed," as in the King James Version, but an active "I am pressing" *('ānōkī mē'īq)*. This definitely rules out any translation beginning, "I am pressed." Kittel suggests the insertion of *'erets* (earth) following "I am pressing," although without textual support.[16] If this is done the translation would read, "Behold, I am causing (the earth) to creak beneath you, just as the fallen grain filling the cart causes the cart to creak." It would seem that the best solution, presenting fewer difficulties, is to follow the suggestion of Kittel, and either emend the text by the addition of *'erets* (earth) or to understand it for the object, although unexpressed. Punishment by earthquake is suggested at other points in Amos (cf. 8:8; 1:1).

Israel is to perish because of her rejection of God, 2:14-16a.— Just as he saw the national origin of Israel as the result of God's activity, Amos also saw the hand of God in her inevitable doom. In a series of vivid portraits, the destruction of the nation is deline-

---

[16] Rudolf Kittel (ed.), *Biblia Hebraica* (Stuttgart: Privileg. Wurtt. Bibel-anstalt, 1959), III, 918.

ated. Those men in Israel epitomizing the physically powerful, the militarily capable, and the courageous of heart are each shown in full flight and helpless terror before the might of God's judgment.

"Flight shall perish from the swift," said the prophet, "and the strong shall not retain his strength, nor shall the mighty save his life." The judgment of God is not in the category of that which can be physically escaped. No matter how swift of foot one may be, judgment inevitably overtakes the individual. The strength of the individual, whether great or small, is of inconsequential effect when he confronts the strength of God. The might of man, says the prophet, is incomparable in its insignificance and will not enable any individual to save himself through a display of his own power.

The one "who handles the bow shall not stand" for the ability of the archer is not the area of judgment. The fear which he strikes in the heart of opposing troops is not to be found in the heart of God. The swift-footed soldier, who made up the bulk of Israel's army, would not be able to save himself in the day when God shakes the earth like a cart loaded with sheaves shakes the earth, for "he who is swift of foot shall not save himself." Not even the cavalryman, the elite of the ancient army, will save his life on that day when God acts. For the prophet proclaimed, "nor shall he who rides the horse save his life." The cavalryman, along with the charioteer, was the most menacing individual in all the armies of the east. As such, if any one had been beyond the reach of God he should have been. Yet, even he must reckon with the certainty of judgment. To every form of the military the prophet announced the inevitability of judgment. Preparation must take place in some field other than this, since even military might will not stand in the hour of testing.

The prophet has much to say to twentieth-century society. While it would be foolish to disparage preparedness against possible military attack; one must, at the same time, recognize that there is no "absolute weapon" other than the human heart, achieving the potentialities God intended for man. If Amos clarified any one issue, he did so in connection with the undue reliance upon the military, whether it be the archer, the foot soldier, or the cavalryman.

Turning to those who were most courageous in the land, Amos observed that even "he who is stout of heart among the mighty shall flee away naked in that day." To find oneself naked before others, whether literally or in terms of the loss of armor, represented the height of humiliation for the ancient Hebrew. Such an experience was mentioned by the editor of the book of Kings, where the cause for the hostilities between Israel and the Ammonites stemmed from the treatment of David's representatives.

So Hanun took David's servants, and shaved off half the beard of each, and cut off their garments in the middle, at their hips, and sent them away. When it was told David, he sent to meet them, for the men were greatly ashamed. And the king said, "Remain at Jericho until your beards have grown, and then return" (2 Sam. 10:4-5).

Israel's fate is settled by the power of God's authority, 2:16b.— Judgment such as that depicted by Amos could not be grounded in human authority. How could it triumph over the best of Israel's men, as the prophet indicated that it would? The prophet could speak with finality concerning judgment, and on that note brought the entire message of doom to a conclusion with the words, "Says the Lord" (2:16b).

The fate of Israel was settled not by virtue of the prophet's power or the might of alien armies. It was settled because of God's action. What Amos said bore the indelible stamp of God's authority. The prophets were never men who spoke only their own words. They were heralds who spoke for God. Although their message was characterized by the thought patterns of the day, the world view of eighth-century Israel, and numerous other human factors, it remained the word which had come from God. It was on the authority of "thus saith the Lord" that the prophets demanded a hearing.

When Amos stood before Israel he spoke the message of God with the power of God. Men might respond either positively or negatively. They might repent and turn to God, as some no doubt did. Or, they might try and run him out of town as did Amaziah (7:12-13). Concerning this they exercised some choice and brought their own powers of decision into play. But in regard to the authority of the prophet's message they had no control, and as Ezekiel was to say in a later day, "Whether they hear or refuse to hear (for they are a rebellious house) they will know that there has been a prophet among them" (2:4-5). When Amos spoke, it was upon the authority of "thus saith the Lord." Because of this, the fate of Israel was sealed.

Having come to the very center of the circle of the nations, Amos concluded the indictment of Israel as he had done in the case of the foreign nations and Judah. Israel must now give account as must every man for his response to God's love. Despite the varied revelation of that love, Israel responded negatively and God in reaction could do nothing other than come in judgment. Here, again, one confronts the pathos of a wasted life and a rejected love. This is the tragedy of a people who knew the high way, but who followed the low. Here, to a greater or lesser degree, is a commentary upon every man's life.

Even as they etched themselves into the very fabric of the lives of those who heard him speak; the caustic, acrid words of Amos burn and sear the soul of the contemporary reader. Like hot metal upon quivering flesh, they brand every man a rebel before God. The words to Damascus and Gaza, Tyre and Edom, Ammon and Moab speak not only to them of a common conscience which had been compromised. They rise up and cause us to face the stark reality that we also have violated that conscience which inheres in the heart of every man.

With living reality the words of the prophet march across the years to wedge themselves into our own hearts, reminding us that we, like Judah, have sinned against the law of God on far more occasions than we care to admit. Like a specter in the night, the awareness of our own rebellions against the matchless love of God haunts us each day of life. Then we see that the words of Amos are words to us; that God's love is more profaned today than it ever was by the ancient Israelite. This is the enduring message of Amos.

4

Responsibility and Privilege
Amos 3:1-15

It was solely through the grace of God that Israel attained as no other nation a privileged position in the world. Because of this manifestation of grace and love, she held a unique responsibility before God. Privilege is with purpose, however, and no nation or individual can afford to forget that the corollary of privilege is responsibility.

Nevertheless, it seems inevitable that man in his sin and ingratitude tends to corrupt the privileges which come to him. He corrupts them by looking upon their reality as an expression of favoritism by God, or by feeling that he is intrinsically better than the less fortunate. This abiding characteristic of man is enmeshed in the social structure of every age. Whether it be an individual of unique talent and ability, or a person who has been blessed above others in a material fashion, the insidious temptation is that of developing an attitude of superiority because of privileges which have come in life.

This was certainly the evil of Amos' day. Failure to see clearly the fact that responsibility naturally follows privilege brought about the downfall of the nation. It will do the same for any nation or any individual—ancient or modern. One cannot enjoy a privileged position without accepting responsibility.

To combat this corrupting evil and to proclaim the message of God concerning it, Amos addressed Israel with a threefold message (3:1-15). With candor and courage Amos indicated: (1) that responsibility goes with privilege (3:1-2), (2) the revelation of God's purposes concerning the privileged (3:3-8), and (3) the result of God's judgment (3:9-11).

Responsibility: The Corollary of Privilege, 3:1-2

The reality of Israel's privileged position is the recurring theme of the lawgiver, historian, psalmist, and prophet alike. Yet, this privilege was not in terms of the externalities of life. Measured in these terms, Israel was an insignificant nation of the ancient Near East. Except for those times when, because of a political vacuum, there were simply no major powers to be found on the scene, Israel was a politically impotent nation. The conquests of a David or an Omri could not equal those of Hammurabi, Thutmose III, or Tiglath-pileser.

The culture of Israel was younger by two millennia than that of either the Tigris-Euphrates or the Nile civilizations. Her literature followed the climactic era of both Egypt and Mesopotamia, and in art forms she never succeeded in producing articles of competitive worth. Indeed, archaeologists have discovered that Israelite conquest inevitably brought deterioration in the quality of pottery and related objects. Her land was small, wedged between the desert and the sea, and seldom produced more than a marginal living for her people. Although to a Bedouin accustomed to a borderland existence, Israel seemed to be a land vertiably flowing with milk and honey, the privileged status of Israel did not lie in the externalities of life. But time had a way of erasing the insignificant, leaving only the glory that was Israel's.

If not in externalities, wherein did the privileged position of Israel reside? Unquestionably, Israel's position was one of privilege because of her unique knowledge of Yahweh—knowledge shared in the covenant experience. It was in terms of communion with him that Israel entered into such a position: privileged in that she was the first of many nations to know him; privileged also in that she was to become the medium whereby other nations would receive that knowledge. "Nowhere is it taught in the Old Testament that God chose Israel because of her inherent greatness," stresses H. H. Rowley, "yet there are passages where it is held that Israel's greatness lies in the fact that God chose her. Nations shall honour her because she is His people, and therefore in honouring her they will really honour him."[1]

---

[1] *The Biblical Doctrine of Election* (London: Lutterworth Press, 1950), p. 19.

To Israel there came this unique privilege of becoming the people through whom God would redeem the world. In the succeeding days which followed the awareness of that choice there were times when Israel sank to unbelievable depths in her lack of faith. But there were also times when she attained heights of glory in her encounter with Yahweh. In all that transpired, Israel existed as the people of God, conscious to a greater or lesser degree of a divine mission and purpose in life which gave her both motivation and direction. Israel's glory was not in the passing pomp and splendor of mighty armies, nor in a culture rivaling others of the East, but in her privileged position and significant responsibility.

Privilege Inherent in Election, 3:1

The privileged status of Israel was in that she had been chosen or elected. One should understand the word in the sense of a choice for service rather than with the connotation of a rigid predetermination of eternal destiny. It was in the context of such a chosen or elected people that Amos could say:

Hear this word which Yahweh has spoken against you, Sons of Israel, upon all the clans which I caused to go up from the land of Egypt (3:1).

Exodus constituted the keystone of Israel's election.—Although, "we can find no period in her history when Israel did not believe that she was the chosen people of Yahweh,"[2] Israel's election was understood by the prophets in terms of the Exodus experience. C. R. North has observed, "If the prophets knew of any covenant with Abraham they do not mention it." [3] There are passages in the Old Testament that make reference to an election under the patriarchs (cf. Gen. 12:1 ff.; 15:7 ff.), and even the prophets know of such a calling, but they mention no covenant (cf. Isa. 41:8 ff.; 51:2; Mic. 7:20). Of the two traditions—one making the Exodus primary, the other isolating the patriarchial calling as central—the Exodus tradition apparently is the older.[4]

---

[2] John Bright, *The Kingdom of God* (New York: Abingdon-Cokesbury Press, 1953), p. 27.

[3] *The Old Testament Interpretation of History* (London: The Epworth Press, 1946), p. 50.

[4] Rowley, *The Biblical Doctrine of Election, op. cit.,* p. 19.

The prophets continually made the totality of the Exodus experience, not the patriarchal call, the keystone of election. This does not deny the validity of both experiences, nor does it say that the prophets did not believe that the patriarchs had been called in an elected sense of service. It is to say, and quite strongly, that when the total scope of Israelite history was surveyed, the event that stood out above the others was the Exodus experience. This included the mighty deliverance of Israel from Egypt with all its attendant phenomena, plus the covenant experience. Hosea agreed with Amos at this point, saying, "When Israel was a child, I loved him, and out of Egypt I called my son" (Hos. 11:1). Ezekiel underscored this in another century, saying, "Thus says the Lord God: On the day when I chose Israel, I swore to the seed of the house of Jacob, making myself known to them in the land of Egypt, I swore to them, saying, I am the Lord your God" (Ezek. 20:5).

It was not the sight of parted waters through which the fleeing slaves passed that supremely impressed Israel, nor the startling events which accompanied that deliverance, although neither was ever forgotten. In the wide scope of history, the continually amazing deed and the most significant reality of the experience was the grace of God made known at the Exodus. For centuries, as they came annually to bring their gifts to the Lord, Israelite men testified to the importance of the Exodus experience, saying,

A wandering Aramean was my father; and he went down into Egypt and sojourned there, few in number; and there he became a nation, great, mighty, and populous. And the Egyptians treated us harshly, and afflicted us, and laid upon us hard bondage. Then we cried to the Lord the God of our fathers, and the Lord heard our voice, and saw our affliction, our toil, and our oppression; and the Lord brought us out of Egypt with a mighty hand and an outstretched arm, with great terror, with signs and wonders; and he brought us into this place and gave us this land, a land flowing with milk and honey (Deut. 26:5-9).

Israel never forgot her humble beginnings, and she never ceased to marvel at what God had done in her midst. For Israel, her election and, indeed, national existence was to be found in the Exodus experience. As Amos said, Israel consisted of "all the clans which I caused to go up out of the land of Egypt." The Exodus remained the keystone of election.

Election comprised the basis of Israel's position.—The unique election of Israel as the people of God was vividly portrayed in: (1) the vocabulary which described this experience, (2) the figures of speech utilized to characterize the nature of her privileged position. Both of these emphases are quite important for a proper understanding of Israel's position of privilege.

One of the most instructive words used concerning the election of Israel is the word *qānāh* (get, acquire). It is often used in the sense of purchasing an object in the ordinary course of life. For example: (1) "When you *buy* a Hebrew slave" (Ex. 21:2), (2) "Only the land of the priests he did not *buy*" (Gen. 47:22), and (3) "The cave of the field at Mach-pelah, to the east of Mamre, which Abraham *bought* with the field from Ephron" (Gen. 50:13).

In the election-covenant experience, Yahweh bought Israel as his own. Of this Moses and the people of Israel could sing, "till thy people, O Lord, pass by, till the people pass by whom thou hast *purchased*" (Ex. 15:16). In expressing the future hope of Israel, Isaiah could say, "In that day the Lord will extend his hand *yet a second time to recover* (*qānāh*, get, acquire) the remnant which is left of his people" (11:11). Yahweh, according to Isaiah, will "in that day" do "yet a second time" for the remnant that which Yahweh had done initially—redeem them through purchase.

Other passages reflecting this phase of God's elective action are: Deuteronomy 32:6, "Is not he your father, who *created* you [Hebrew text has, *qānāh*—get, acquire], who made you and established you" and Psalm 74:2, "Remember thy congregation, which thou hast *gotten* of old."

The action of God in choosing Israel was like that of an individual who went into the market place and purchased an object. A man who bought a slave, or an individual who acquired a burial cave, had carried out the same type of action which Yahweh did in the purchase of Israel. Acquired through *creation*, acquired through *preservation*, and acquired supremely through elective *redemption*; Israel was his in election because Yahweh had purchased her.

Yahweh not only acquired or purchased Israel, he also chose her (*bāchar*). This word is used approximately fifty-one times in the Old Testament in connection with a choice made on the part of Yahweh. Of these occurrences approximately thirty-four are concerned with the divine choice of individuals or groups. The classic statement on the choice of Israel is to be found in the reminder of the Deuteronomist that, "It was not because you were more in number than any other people that the Lord set his love upon you and *chose* you, for you were the fewest of all peoples" (7:7). Again, it is used of Abraham when it was said, "Thou art the Lord, the God who didst *choose* Abram and bring him forth out of Ur of the Chaldees and give him the name Abraham" (Neh. 9:7). Other passages refer to the servant (Isa. 44:1), the seed of the patriarchs (Deut. 4:37; 10:15), Levites (Deut. 18:5), Aaron (Psalm 105:26), Judah (1 Chron. 28:4), the king (Deut. 17:15), and especially David (1 Sam. 16:8-10).[5]

Amos himself utilized the third word characteristically used of Israel's election—*yādha'*, saying, "You only have I *known* of all the families of the earth" (3:2). The same word is used in Hosea 5:3, "I know Ephraim, and Israel is not hid from me." Since the word will be considered in greater detail in the treatment of Amos 3:2, no further consideration of it will be made at this time, except to say that it is one of the most graphic words used to depict the election experience.

Not only in vocabulary but in figures of speech alike, election was vividly depicted. Especially was this true in the parallel figures of fatherhood and marriage. Hosea could say of Israel, "When Israel was a child, I loved him, and out of Egypt I called my son" (Hos. 11:1). In moving words he depicted the marvelous grace of God in Israel's early days by saying, "Yet it was I who taught Ephraim to walk, I took them up in my arms" (Hos. 11:3). Isaiah made use of the same expression to say, "Sons have I reared and brought up, but they have rebelled against me" (Isa. 1:2), and Moses could say to Pharoah, "Thus says the Lord, Israel is my first-born son" (Ex. 4:22).

Hosea depicted the relationship between Israel and Yahweh in terms of marriage and of Israel's future could say:

Therefore, behold, I will allure her,
  and bring her into the wilderness,
  and speak tenderly to her.

---

[5] *Cf.* Francis Brown, S. R. Driver, and Charles A. Briggs, *A Hebrew and English Lexicon* (Oxford: The Clarendon Press, 1959), pp. 103 f.

58 AMOS AND HIS MESSAGE

And there I will give her her vineyards,
    and make the valley of Achor a door of hope.
And there she shall answer as in the days of her youth,
    as at the time when she came out of the land of Egypt (2:14-15).

Jeremiah was later to make much the same emphasis in saying,

> I remember the devotion of your youth,
>   your love as a bride,
> How you followed me in the wilderness,
>   in a land not sown.
> Israel was holy to the Lord,
>   the first fruits of his harvest.
> All who ate of it became guilty;
>   evil came upon them,
> says the Lord (2:2-3).

It was, indeed, election that comprised the basis for Israel's position of privilege, and through a series of movingly graphic words and figures that election is depicted in the Old Testament. The election is as much a reality as is a purchase *(qānāh)*, a choice that has been made *(bāchar)*, or knowledge that has been acquired *(yādha‘)*. The relationship of Israel to Yahweh is that of both a dutiful son, begotten in love, and a faithful, devoted wife, called from a far country and protected in days of marriage. Israel's privileged position rested solely in that type of election relationship. As E. C. Rust observes,

His relation to [Israel] is not one of quasi-natural necessity but one of moral choice. Its continued existence is not necessary for His own being, nor does he depend upon its exaltation for the maintenance of His own honor. . . . this election is grounded in redemptive choice.[6]

Extension of judgment to Israel is contingent upon election.—As strange as it may seem, the extension of judgment to Israel was directly contingent upon the fact that she was the elect of God, the Chosen People, the potential kingdom of God on earth. Election meant judgment; for although Yahweh had chosen Israel, "this did not mean, as they supposed, that they had a monopoly of the divine

---

[6] "Old Testament Theology" (Mimeographed, Southern Baptist Theological Seminary, Louisville, Kentucky, 1953), p. 39.

favor. It did not mean that they would certainly escape when the
day of judgment came. It simply meant moral opportunity."[7] Herein
is contained the heart of Israel's responsibility within the election-
covenant relationship—"it simply meant moral opportunity." Israel
could have become God's medium of revelation to the entire world.
Rejecting and denying this "moral opportunity" brought the judgment of God.

As the wise man of Israel observed: "My son, do not despise
the Lord's discipline or be weary of his reproof, for the Lord reproves him whom he loves, as a father the son in whom he delights"
(Prov. 3:11-12). The writer of Hebrews made use of this by saying,
"If you are left without discipline, in which all have participated,
then you are illegitimate children and not sons" (Heb. 12:8). There
exists no finer example of the sonship of Israel than the judgment
of God coming as he sought to purify Israel by the removal of the
dross and the chaff. Election is for judgment as well as for service.

Elected or chosen for judgment—this is a frightful understanding
of the election-covenant experience, but it is an abiding principle
that runs throughout all of God's redemptive activity. Yet, it is not
so frightful as it is consoling, for without judgment there would
be little if any repentance. Without repentance there could be no
redemption. Luthi has observed that some men "proclaim judgment
as if God's judgment upon our sin had as its aim to bring us woe!
The Word of God, however, which names and counts and weighs
the sin of man, seeks to bring man good fortune. It is a severe kind
of good fortune, but it is good fortune to believe in a God who is
not disposed to be too lenient."[8]

Privilege Implicit in Knowledge, 3:2a

Not only was the privileged position of Israel implicit in her
election, but the knowledge of God was hers because God had
chosen her. Amos, in seeking to bring Israel to accept her responsibilities as the chosen of God, reminded her on behalf of Yahweh,
"You only have I known of all the families of the earth" (3:2a).

The prophet certainly is not to be understood in the sense that
God had demonstrated no awareness of other nations. In a later

---

[7] Knudson, *op. cit.*, p. 78.
[8] *Op. cit.*, p. 29.

section Amos stressed God's universal activity in these startling words: "Are you not like the Ethiopians to me, O people of Israel?" says the Lord. "Did I not bring up Israel from the land of Egypt, and the Philistines from Caphtor and the Syrians from Kir" (9:7). In light of this it would be impossible to maintain without fallacy that God had concerned himself with no other nations. Exclusivism of this type was not the prophet's purpose. Israel alone had been known of God, however, in the sense of personal, intimate knowledge such as would constitute the veritable self-revelation of God. The prophet was correct in emphasizing that God had entered into no such relationship with other nations.

The word "known" was used much in the sense that it is in some contexts in life today. Often, one will hear the question—"Do you know such and such a person?" To this there is given the answer— "I have met him but I do not actually know him." This is the personal, intimate knowledge that Amos had in mind in 3:2a.

The word translated "known" is the Hebrew verb yādha', and is customarily translated "know." It is not in the root meaning of this word that insight is given so much as through its usage. Although it is quite often used in the sense of knowledge of the most general type (1 Sam. 22:15; Jer. 38:24; etc.), it is also used of the most personal and intimate knowledge possible. In this connection it is often used as a euphemism for sexual relations. For example: "Now Adam knew Eve his wife, and she conceived and bore Cain" (Gen. 4:1); "The maiden was very fair to look upon, a virgin, whom no man had known" (Gen. 24:16); or finally, "The maiden was very beautiful; and she became the king's nurse and ministered to him; but the king knew her not" (1 Kings 1:4).

It was with such knowledge as this that Yahweh "knew" Israel, knowledge of the most intimate and personal type imaginable. As Gwynn observes, this was knowledge used "of Abraham (Gen. xviii. 19), 'I have known him, to the end that he may command his children that they may keep the way of Jehovah'; of Israel (Hosea xiii. 5), 'I did know thee in the wilderness.' Cf. Ps. 1:6 'The Lord knoweth the way of the righteous,' xxxi. 7, 'Thou hast known my soul in adversities,' cxliv. 3, 'What is man, that thou takest knowledge of him?' "[9]

---

[9] *Op. cit.*, p. 14.

Even in the face of such intimate knowledge as this there is no sense of discrimination. The purpose of Yahweh in granting knowledge of himself is never that it might be kept within the confines of the fellowship which receives it. Instead, it is his purpose that this knowledge be shared, in turn, with all men. The problem, if it may be called such, of Israel knowing God in such an intimate manner while others did not, is thereby alleviated considerably. For God to touch the world at any point necessitated his beginning his work through a particular people. It was never the intention of God that this knowledge be limited. For, said the prophet, "the earth shall be full of the knowledge of the Lord as the waters cover the sea" (Isa. 11:9). The ideal of God was to be realized, said Jeremiah, in that "no longer shall each man teach his neighbor and each his brother, saying, 'Know the Lord,' for they shall all know me, from the least of them to the greatest, says the Lord" (Jer. 31:34).

Intimate knowledge of an experiential nature began with Israel, but it was not intended to end there. It was the will of God that such knowledge be extended to all men. In this concept any thought of favoritism is removed, for the only reason that Israel's intimate knowledge of God existed was to be found in the sharing of that knowledge.

Privilege Implies Responsibility, 3:2b

"You only have I known of all the families of the earth," said the prophet, "therefore I will punish you for all your iniquities" (3:2). "Starting from the same premises," says a prominent writer, "Amos reached a conclusion diametrically opposite to theirs, because his conception of the character of God was a whole world apart from theirs."[10] In the mind of the people Yahweh was inseparably bound to them because of the ties of the election-covenant experience. Thus, the conviction prevailed that God would not only bless, but that he would never come in judgment because they were the chosen of God. With this Amos stood in unalterable opposition. It was his unshakable conviction that special privilege meant special responsibility.

H. H. Rowley clearly states the biblical doctrine of election in a

---

[10] McFayden, *op. cit.*, p. 25.

book by that title. In the course of its development he stresses that election is always for service. Such service was a natural corollary of election, not only for Israel as a group, but for individuals both within and without the covenant (cf. Cyrus, Isa. 45:1). In seeking to underscore the immediate relevancy of this in the individual Israelite's life, Rowley says,

It could not be made clearer that here there is no conception of God being tied to Israel willy-nilly, so that whatever Israel cared to do He was bound to back her. Her election was not something automatic that made her His people for all time by mere physical generation. She entered into the Covenant voluntarily, and each generation must renew it by accepting for itself its obligations, or it would place itself outside the covenant.[11]

Election and covenant both involved the surrender of the individual Israelite to the demands of that experience, a surrender that inevitably involved service. The entire matter of covenant responsibility can be summed up in the precept formulated later by another Prophet, "Every one to whom much is given, of him will much be required; and of him to whom men commit much they will demand the more" (Luke 12:48). The "much" that Israel had received through her position of privilege among the nations meant that more would be required of her.

With somber words of deep reality Amos declared to the people of his own blood the message of God that flowed through his veins. The depth of his conviction could be matched only by the relevancy of his message as he confronted Israel with her responsibility before God. These words must have cut and pierced as they found their mark:

Hear this word that the Lord has spoken against you, O people of Israel, against the whole family which I brought up out of the land of Egypt:
> You only have I known
>   of all the families of the earth;
>   therefore I will punish you
>   for all your iniquities (3:1-2).

The prophet has much to say to modern men privileged to live in a free nation while millions reside behind the Iron and Bamboo

---

[11] *The Biblical Doctrine of Election, op. cit.*, pp. 47-48.

Curtains. The prophetic voice still echoes upon the contemporary North American family who is better fed, better clothed, and better housed than ninety per cent of the people in the world and who does not assume the corollary of privilege—responsibility. The thunder still rolls and the voice of the prophet still rumbles upon men who accept the privilege of equal opportunity in a free society, but who are willing to pawn off second-class citizenship upon multitudes of racial minority groups.

The notes of the prophetic message still reverberate upon those who accept all that God has given in every area of life, but cast a blind eye upon the sight of inevitable responsibilities and turn a deaf ear to the voice of God as it seeks to call men back to their covenantal obligations. The death bell still tolls for the individual, the church, or the nation that will not respond positively, since privilege does involve responsibility.

Revelation of God's Purposes Concerning the Privileged, 3:3-8

Toward what future did the Chosen People move? What were the purposes of God for them? How can man know the will of God? Many answers might be suggested in response to the latter question, but among them must certainly be found the prophetic ministry of God-called men. Israel should obviously know the purposes of God says Amos, for there is a principle of cause and effect which is operative in all of life. Every "effect" produced in life has its ultimate cause. The casual explanation for the words of the prophet stems from the fact that God has spoken to the prophet concerning Israel. Israel can know the will of God because it has been given to the prophet, who in turn proclaims that word with uncompromised integrity and undivided loyalty.

Certainty of Cause and Effect as a Principle in Life, 3:3-6

Nothing happens in life without an ultimate cause, stressed Amos. Whether it be man and his appointment, a lion and its prey, a trap and its catch, the trumpet and its alarm, or judgment and God's activity, nothing occurs apart from casual forces. This is apparent in the declaration of the one who said:

> Do two walk together,
>   unless they have made an appointment?

> Does a lion roar in the forest,
>   when he has no prey?
> Does a young lion cry out from his den,
>   if he has taken nothing?
> Does a bird fall in a snare on the earth,
>   when there is no trap for it?
> Does a snare spring up from the ground,
>   when it has taken nothing?
> Is a trumpet blown in a city,
>   and the people are not afraid?
> Does evil befall a city,
>   unless the Lord has done it? (3:3-6).

There is a pattern of cause and effect discernable in all of life lifting all existence beyond the area of haphazard chance into the area of immediate, casual responsibility. An inexorable law controls every area of life—moral, spiritual, or physical. If judgment falls, as it inevitably shall, its reason is to be discovered in the action of the Lord. Likewise, when the prophet speaks, the cause is not hard to find. It is to be discovered in the stirring of God within the prophet's heart. Because of this, Israel could know with certainty that which God purposed for his Chosen People.

Communication Through Cause and Effect, 3:7

Communication from Yahweh to the people was made through that same principle of cause and effect, for "surely the Lord God does nothing, without revealing his secret to his servants the prophets" (3:7). Two emphases of startling import were interwoven with the prophetic message at this point. First, the patience and grace of God was strangely revealed in that God "does nothing without revealing his secret." Second, judgment did not fall without warning, and every man had adequate revelation to come to repentance and restoration.

Not only was communication made, but it came through the prophets who were supremely his servants. It was to the prophet that Israel looked for God's word of judgment and grace, of rebuke and restoration. Otto Baab says concerning the communication of the divine will through the prophetic ministry:

He [the prophet] preached to a people which he loved as only a Hebrew steeped in its splendid history and heroic traditions can love. He preached against the people of his love as only a man consumed with the fires of God's justice can preach when faced with cruelty and iniquity. . . . He was a man of tension and strife, forced to oppose his people that God might save them.[12]

The principle is eternal. "The Lord God does nothing, without revealing his secret to his servants the prophets" (3:7). Surely in view of this, the constant call must be for men who will truly become his servants and upon hearing that divine word, proclaim it with courage, honesty, and integrity. This should be the effective cause of every contemporary prophet—divine activity in the human heart.

Consequences of Cause and Effect for Israel and the Prophet, 3:8

If there was a divine cause at work producing certain effects in society, what were the effects of that power? Amos stressed that there were consequences: first, for Israel; second, for the prophet himself.

"The lion has roared; who will not fear?" With startling words whose implications could not be overlooked, the prophet introduced Israel to the first consequence of the principle of cause and effect. The Lion, Yahweh himself, had already roared in anticipated judgment. Who among the people would not fear? Amos often had heard the roar of the lion in the wilderness. Hearing his roar, he knew once again that a helpless, weak sheep had fallen prey to its foe. "The doom is certain," says Snaith, "when the lion roars, he is already leaping on the prey. The punishment is already in process; it is now inevitable and cannot be turned back (1:6,9,11, etc.).[13]

The voice of the lion's roar does more than speak to Israel of its inevitable judgment. It also calls the prophet with a magnetic appeal that cannot be stifled, driving him forward with an impelling force that cannot be suppressed. Here is found not only the proper motivation but the sustaining power for the prophetic ministry and message: "The Lord God has spoken; who can but prophesy?" In a time of confused motivations and misdirected ministries, Amos has much to say to the contemporary, prophetic minister. As Baab clearly and forcefully states:

[12] *Op. cit., pp.* 20-21.
[13] *Op. cit.,* p. 12.

These men did not answer the call of duty or of conscience, the call of country or of community. They responded to the call of God. . . . This fact alone explains their peculiar passion and their program of preaching in perilous times. It stands in sharp contrast to much that is piously and politely described as a "call" today. What is now often simply one's choice of a career or submission to social pressure appears feeble alongside the prophet's call. He was deeply convinced that it came directly and decisively from God.[14]

Result of God's Judgment, 3:9-15

In the face of fiery words depicting the inexorable law of cause and effect, one should never forget that "this is no . . . nomad's hatred of cities and of the culture of settled men. It is not a temper; it is a vision of history."[15] The message of Amos was, indeed, a vision of history. In the course of history, what would the inevitable law of cause and effect bring forth upon Israel? With pungent, powerful declarations the prophet sets forth three effects of such judgment.

Irresponsible Conduct Matched with Irresistible Judgment, 3:9-11

At this point Amos did something unheard of, for "never once, as far as we know," says Milley, "did a predecessor of Amos bring a message of doom from Yahweh either for the nations or for Israel herself."[16] With a keen consciousness of the social conditions which existed in his own day, Amos declared that upon such irresponsible conduct there would come irresistible judgment. The prophet was aware of the fact that, in the light of the situations which existed, judgment must come. Israel's conduct provided no other alternative or response on God's part.

Call to the nations as witnesses, 3:9.—It was not Judah lying to the south that Amos called forth as a witness. It was not even the righteous, who doubtless remained in Israel, who were summoned to observe the depth of Israel's sin. Rather, it was the nations outside the circle of either Judah or Israel who were called upon by the prophet to serve as witnesses of Israel's depravity and irresponsible conduct.

---

[14] *Op. cit.,* p. 17.

[15] G. A. Smith, *op. cit.,* p. 152.

[16] C. Ross Milley, *The Prophets of Israel* (New York: Philosophical Library, 1959), p. 36.

Proclaim to the strongholds in Ashdod [17]
   and to the strongholds in the land of Egypt,
and say, "Assemble yourselves upon the mountains of Samaria,
   and see the great tumults within her,
   and the oppressions in her midst" (3:9).

"There is something awful," says Mitchell, "in the thought that
the sins of the chosen people have reached such a degree of gross-
ness that Jehovah can safely rely upon strangers to his grace to
approve any penalty he may decree."[18] To speak so forthrightly on
the nature of her sin was startling enough, but to indicate that non-
covenantal nations were to be called as witnesses to observe her
depravity was both infuriating and demoralizing to Israel. The
fact that ancient enemies of Israel—Egypt, whose tyranny was well
remembered from the Exodus experience, and the Philistines
(epitomized in "Ashdod"), whose marauding raids were a threat
to the early monarchy—were called as witnesses made the words of
Amos more galling than ever. Such action on the part of the prophet
is indicative of the depths to which Israel had fallen.

At a later day Egypt and Ashdod would no doubt have been
included among the "Gentiles who have not the law [but] do by
nature what the law requires" (Rom. 2:14). At least their condemnation was less than that of Israel, since they sinned in ignorance of the law while both Israel and Judah sinned with the full
awareness of God's self-revelation. It is a singular condemnation
when nations without the knowledge of God (Amos 3:2) can be
called as witnesses upon the people of God who have compromised
and violated that knowledge.

Conduct produced by a lack of knowledge, 3:10.—The contributory cause for such conduct was not difficult to find. " 'They do not
know how to do right,' says the Lord, 'those who store up violence
and robbery in their strongholds' " (3:10). Knowledge of God is

---

[17] The Septuagint, followed at this point by the RSV, reads "Assyria," not
Ashdod. Ashdod was not a threat to the nation in the time of Amos and for
this reason Assyria may well have been intended. The reading "Ashdod" has
been retained, however, on the hypothesis that Amos sought to chasten Israel
by portraying their traditional enemies, the Philistines, as Israel's judge. It is
not likely that Amos intended to imply that Ashdod or the Philistines were a
threat in the eighth century. His reference was entirely a literary device.
[18] H. G. Mitchell, *Amos: An Essay in Exegesis* (rev. ed.; Boston; Houghton
Mifflin Co., 1900), p. 26.

always the object or goal of the covenantal experience. But such knowledge inevitably involves more than mystical contemplation upon God carried out in a secluded sanctuary. It is concerned, rather, with the totality of man's being, thus directly related to the knowledge of "how to do right." The knowledge of God is inextricably interwoven with the social involvements of man. No amount of superficial professions and acts of ritual will supplant experiential knowledge of God, translated into daily involvement in one's own social structure. The prophets were of one mind and spoke with one voice upon this. Hosea agreed with Amos by saying, "My people are destroyed for lack of knowledge" (4:6); knowledge, says Amos, of "how to do right."[19]

Such failure in knowing "how to do right" had numerous implications, summed up by the phrase, "those who store up violence and robbery in their strongholds." Already Amos had characterized them as people with "great tumults" and "oppression" (3:9). The present indictment served only to underscore their irresponsible conduct as the people of God. They were people who did violence, stored up robbery, and carried out one oppression after another. This is the inevitable course of every society that either forgets or forsakes its knowledge of God, upon which the knowledge to do right is based.

Certainty of judgment in history, 3:11.—"Therefore," because of such irresponsible conduct, "thus says the Lord God: 'An adversary shall surround the land, and bring down your defences from you, and your strongholds shall be plundered'" (3:11). "The higher the dam is piled, the deeper the water that is gathered behind it," said Maclaren, "and the surer and more destructive the flood when it bursts. Long-delayed judgments are severe in proportion as they are slow."[20] The dam had, indeed, been piled high in Israel, and the waters stored up in destructive judgment were soon to come cascading down in devastating vengeance because of the enormity of Israel's sin.

---

[19] "Right" as used here is from the word *nākhah* (straight, right), the root idea of which means "be in front of." The word has the idea of straightforwardness. That which is "right" is out in front for all to see, not hidden away.

[20] Alexander Maclaren, *The Books of Ezekiel, Daniel, and the Minor Prophets* ("Expositions of Holy Scripture" [New York: A. C. Armstrong & Son, 1909]), p. 155.

One should read such passages as this with bifocal vision. One part of the vision should be cast upon the words of the prophet before the mid-eighth century; the other part focused with clarity upon the last quarter of the same century, when the invading Assyrian powers overwhelmed the Northern Kingdom and carried away captive the flower of its society. As Skinner observes, "The prophet's mind is the seismograph of providence, vibrating to the first faint tremors that herald the coming earthquake."[21]

The unanimous testimony of the prophets, regardless of the era of their ministry, emphasizes the activity of God in history. As mentioned earlier (cf. 1:3 to 2:3), God is never removed from the arena of history, and all order and direction of its movement are within his control. Despite this confidence, the prophets have often recognized the temporary reversals in history as did Matthew Arnold. Possessed by an almost eternal note of sadness, and having witnessed the recession of the "Sea of Faith" as he termed it, he observed of his own era in history:

> Ah, love, let us be true
>   To one another! for the world, which seems
>   To lie before us like a land of dreams,
> So various, so beautiful, so new,
> Hath really neither joy, nor love, nor light,
>   Nor certitude, nor peace, nor help for pain;
>   And we are here as on a darkling plain
> Swept with confused alarms of struggle and flight,
> Where ignorant armies clash by night.
>   MATTHEW ARNOLD

But of the certainty of such a judgment in history, there was no doubt in the mind of Amos. The reality of judgment was so certain that he could use verbs in the "perfect," indicating completed action, to describe the imminent downfall of Israel. The annihilation of the kingdom of Israel was so certain in the mind of the prophet that he spoke of it as having already come to pass. A literal translation of his doom oracle would read, "Therefore thus said Lord Yahweh, 'An adversary and a surrounder of the earth, and he *has brought down* from you your strength, and he *has spoiled* your

---

[21] John Skinner, *Prophecy and Religion* (Cambridge: Cambridge University Press, 1922), p. 38.

palaces'" (3:11). It was with this note of certainty that the prophet
concluded that the irresponsible conduct was to be matched with
irresistible judgment (3:9-11).

Inevitable Judgment Is Tempered with Inexhaustible Mercy, 3:12

The action of God is wonderfully contradictory in that it confronts man with emphases from one extreme to another: wealth
through poverty, exaltation through humiliation, and even life
through death. Such apparent contradictions are manifest on every
hand, but especially at this point in Amos. What would love be
without judgment? Certainly it would represent far less than the
biblical view of divine love which includes the judgment of God.
Conversely, what would judgment be without love? Would it not
degenerate into a type of wrath akin to that of a man who completely loses control of himself and acts with subsequent irresponsibility? The declaration of the prophet asserted that God's judgment,
as inevitable as it may have been, was tempered with mercy. Herein
the grace of God was strangely revealed once again. Who could
have stood had he come in judgment without love. "How [could]
Jacob stand? He is so small!" (7:5).

Judgment destroys a part of those on whom it falls, stressed the
prophet. It was because of such an understanding of God as this
that he could say:

Thus says the Lord: "As the shepherd rescues from the mouth of the
lion two legs, or a piece of an ear, so shall the people of Israel who dwell
in Samaria be rescued, with the corner of a couch and part of a bed"
(3:12).

Amos undoubtedly had in mind the ancient practice of requiring
the shepherd to produce the remains of a sheep in order to demonstrate that he had not appropriated the beast for himself. Jacob
reflected this ancient Near Eastern practice when he said, "That
which was torn by wild beasts I did not bring to you; I bore the
loss of it myself" (Gen. 31:39). Israelite law specified concerning
livestock that "if it is torn by beasts, let him bring it as evidence;
he shall not make restitution for what has been torn" (Ex. 22:13).

The twofold picture is quite clear. When God comes in judgment upon Israel there will be left only two shinbones and part of

an ear. His wrath will descend in such a fashion that all that will be
left of Samaria will be the "corner of a couch and part of a bed."
The inclusive picture of judgment is quite vivid. It falls upon the
city with its couches and its ornate beds, but it also falls upon the
rural shepherd on the mountainsides. This is one side of judgment,
the destructive side that annihilates that which is irresponsible in
its conduct and false to that knowledge which has come concerning
the nature and demands of God.

Judgment delivers a remnant, however, stressed Amos (3:12b).
This is the other side of inevitable judgment, and in the long range
of history it is perhaps just as significant as the former. Despite the
intensity of judgment, there is a part left. Judgment does deliver
a remnant. The body of the sheep was greatly consumed, but even
if only two bones and a piece of ear remained, they would testify
to the fact that all had not been lost. Only a couch and a part of a
bed were rescued from the city, but they were delivered and in this
there was hope. While not stated with the clarity of Amos 5:15, the
idea of a remnant is anticipated, for "so shall the people of Israel
who dwell in Samaria be rescued" (3:12). Judgment would come
but God's mercy gave assurance of a remnant.

Judgment was inevitable for Israel as for every nation and individual. Yet, judgment is always tempered with a mercy that is
inexhaustible. But this should give to no man a license to sin
through the compromising of the life he lives, for even judgment
tempered with mercy is a terrible experience. To temper judgment
with mercy is but to refrain from the complete annihilation of a
people. It is not to say that judgment is not a reality. Herein is the
mystery of God's action: love that means judgment, and judgment
that means mercy.

Indiscriminate Judgment upon the Intentional Sins of Israel, 3:13-15

The judgment of God is indiscriminate in its inclusiveness just as
it is irresistible in its force. It does not fall upon one to the exclusion
of the other. Such discrimination, as so often characterizes man in
human relationships, is a part neither of the character nor of the
purpose of God. In keeping with his nature, fairness and equity are
manifested in his judgment, justice in his grace. Based upon this
are the words of Amos which conclude the third chapter:

> "Hear, and testify against the house of Jacob,"
>   says the Lord God, the God of hosts,
> "that on the day I punish Israel for his transgressions,
>   I will punish the altars of Bethel,
> and the horns of the altar shall be cut off
>   and fall to the ground.
> I will smite the winter house with the summer house;
>   and the houses of ivory shall perish,
> and the great houses shall come to an end,"
>   says the Lord (3:13-15).

Primary among the objects of God's judgment "on the day that I punish Israel" was the religious system of the period. Although instituted through the divine will (cf. the ritual decalogue of Ex. 34:1 ff.; Deut. 12-17; Lev. 1:1 ff.), religious life in the formal and external sense had degenerated. Practically all of the prophets in one way or another denounce some facet of its life—ritual, personnel, or the undue veneration of the site of worship (cf. Jer. 7:1 ff.). It was a part of Amos' burden to pronounce judgment upon the cultic life of his day (cf. 4:4 ff.; 5:21 ff.). This he did without discrimination.

The multiple altars of Bethel were to feel the blast of God's judgment, the very horns themselves being cut off.[22] In this denunciation there was a twofold threat. First, the right of sanctuary would be forfeited. Under this provision an individual could enter in and take hold upon the horns of the altar and claim sanctuary against the wrath of his oppressor. This occurred in the case of Solomon's son of whom it was said, "Adonijah feared Solomon; and he arose, and went, and caught hold of the horns of the altar" (1 Kings 1:50). In the day of God's wrath there will be no sanctuary to which guilty culprits can flee.

Second, the prophet also had in mind the actual destruction that would come in such a time of judgment as he described. The altars themselves would be literally destroyed, although this interpretation is secondary to the loss of sanctuary.

Not only were the altars, symbolic of institutionalized religion,

---

[22] "Originally the skin of the sacrificial victim with horns attached may have been spread on the altar. . . . In later usage, there were four horns, i.e., artificial projections at the four corners of the altar (Ex. 27:2) on which the blood of the victim was smeared (Lev. 4:7)."—Robinson, "Amos," *op. cit.*, p. 779.

to be punished, but the entire social structure as well. " 'I will smite the winter house with the summer house; and the houses of ivory shall perish, and the great houses shall come to an end,' says the Lord" (3:15).

The "winter house with the summer house" has to do not with two separate houses, but with a single house which has an upper story or higher structure for use in hot weather.[23] Such houses constituted a sign of luxury on the part of those who could possess such structures, and their very possession was an evidence of guilt when compared with the undue poverty that existed on every side in Israel. With such structures, epitomizing inordinate wealth, Amos had not the slightest patience. As he viewed the luxury of the upper classes, "even apart from moral issues, he seems to show a certain satisfaction in the prospect of its [luxury] destruction," says H. Wheeler Robinson.[24]

With this symbol of wealth there was also grouped the house of ivory and the great house. The latter is obvious in its meaning. However, the former refers not to houses constructed with ivory, but houses inlaid at certain points with ivory, such as have been discovered in archaeological excavations.[25] These shall perish or be brought to an end, pronounced the prophet, since they represent the outward manifestation of an inward element of greed and selfishness. Unless there is something wrong within the heart, men do not dwell in paneled houses of ivory while others go hungry. It was upon the basis of this principle that Amos indicated that judgment would come upon the houses mentioned.

To men of all ages the prophetic voice of Amos rings forth with undiminished power to proclaim responsibility as the logical corollary of privilege. Israel had attained a position of extreme privilege without assuming her responsibilities. As Hosea said,

> And she did not know
> that it was I who gave her
> the grain, the wine, and the oil,

---

[23] *Ibid.* Some do feel that separate homes are intended. Cf. Cripps, *op. cit.*, p. 164.

[24] *Ibid.*

[25] Cf. the "Megiddo Ivories" as one such example. Discovered at Megiddo, they were obviously inlays which were used in a wealthy era.

> and who lavished upon her silver
>   and gold which they used for Baal.
> Therefore I will take back
>   my grain in its time,
>   and my wine in its season;
> and I will take away my wool and my flax,
>   which were to cover her nakedness (2:8-9).

It was true of Israel that she did receive grain and wine and oil, but most of all knowledge of God. Yet in her response, "she did not know that it was I" who gave it. Completely insensitive to the ultimate source of her blessings and privileges, she ignored not only her responsibilities but God, who had given the privileged position and called her to responsibility.

With deliberate and unabated vigor Amos continues to intone the awful notes of God's judgment upon people who accept a privileged position in a world of physical need and spiritual sickness, but refuse to assume parallel responsibilities. To every man who reads the book with prayerful consideration, Amos' words still come alive. One may cringe within at the awareness of the varied ways in which privilege has been personally corrupted and responsibility knowingly denied. But the Word of God becomes strangely relevant and uncomfortably disturbing to twentieth-century churches.

5

Yet Ye Would Not!
Amos 4:1-13

Personally involved and divinely concerned with the fate of the nation, Amos witnessed an evergrowing avalanche of disasters thundering down the mountainous slopes of Israel. Despite her outward security and prosperity, it was a time of desperate crisis for the nation. Yet, even these crises were turned through prophetic initiative into further opportunities for the manifestation of the relevancy of the prophetic word.

Amos arose in the face of such catastrophes to fulfil the high purpose of his calling, that of relating the events of history to the will of God. Predicting the future was not, as many suppose it to have been, the primary function of the prophet. The supreme task of the prophet was to interpret the events of history in the light of the will and purpose of God. Laboring under the direction of the Spirit of God, the prophets saw the hand of God in the events of daily life. They sought to answer the pressing questions confronted in man's struggle with the totality of life. Such correlation of the divine will and the realities of life is a continuing enterprise, however, and will never be answered short of a perfect apprehension of the full nature of God. It must, therefore, be a continuing quest that embraces every generation.

How was God related to the turbulent events of the world in the time of Amos? What was the relationship between the calamities, the crises, and the disappointments in life to the will of God? Who should bring to man a life in keeping with God's character? How was one to view the will of God when famine existed (4:6) and children were starving? What was the intention of God for man in the presence of drought (8:7-8)—the most feared of all calamities

to agriculturists, modern and ancient? What was the purpose behind the destruction of crops by blight and by insect (4:9) when
the life of ancient man literally depended upon the abundance of
the local crop? How did warfare (4:10-11) with the sound of battle,
the stench of dead bodies, and the shocking thrust of cold metal or
tearing stone fit into the purposes of God? What had God to do
with all of this? The task of the prophet is to answer such questions.

Such correlation of history and the divine will is not a situation
to which modern man can plead lack of concern. It is a crying,
personal problem of present existence. How does one relate the
divine will and the mushrooming cloud over Hiroshima and Naga-
saki—the cloud that overshadows New York, London, Moscow,
and Paris? Is God still in control, or has the world been hijacked
by a mutinous crew who now runs it with a pirate flag at the helm?
This is the continuing task of the prophet, ancient and modern: to
relate the will of a good, just, and holy God to a history that is often
neither good, nor just, nor holy; but in the whirlwind of its own
rebellion consumes the purposes of God the moment they appear.
The world still waits for a prophet to speak. It may or it may not
heed his word, but the battered masses of this breathless and ex-
hausted generation wait for someone to tell them where God is.
The unending and demanding task of every true prophet is that of
relating the conflicting events of history to the will of God. To this
problem Amos speaks. Do the prophets of today continue his urgent
and necessary ministry?

For Amos there was a direct relationship between God's purposes
and the day-by-day events of history. In seeking to understand this
relationship the prophet first considered the primary evils of his
day: a corrupt social system and a degenerate ecclesiasticism.
Then he showed how God had sought through historical processes
to warn his people against such evils. Warnings were not heeded,
however, and in view of the failure of the people to respond to the
historical revelation of God, Amos asserted that judgment must inevitably fall upon Israel.

Two Primary Evils of Amos' Day, 4:1-5

With intuitive insight born of the presence of God, Amos put his
finger upon the throbbing, pulsing heartbeat of Israel's problem.

With the diagnostic skill of a trained physician he interpreted correctly the cause of the nation's ills. Two areas of life were laid bare for all to see: the social and the ecclesiastical. Of the former the prophet could say,

> Hear this word, you cows of Bashan,
>> who are in the mountain of Samaria,
> who oppress the poor, who crush the needy,
>> who say to their husbands, "Bring, that we may drink!" (4:1).

Of the latter he lashed out in like fashion, saying,

> Come to Bethel, and transgress;
>> to Gilgal, and multiply transgression;
> bring your sacrifices every morning,
>> your tithes every three days;
> offer a sacrifice of thanksgiving of that which is leavened,
>> and proclaim freewill offerings, publish them;
>> for so you love to do, O people of Israel! (4:4-5).

Spurred on by the sheer tragedy of the entire situation, Amos emphasized the true source and nature of Israel's degenerate condition.

The Corruption of Israelite Society

The prophets of Israel would give little support to the modern protest that "the church ought to preach the gospel and leave everything else alone." For the prophets, the message of God was so interwoven into the fabric of daily life that the two could not be separated. Indeed, it would be difficult to imagine that greatest of all prophets, Jesus of Nazareth, apart from the social issues of his day. Strip the gospel of Jesus Christ from the context of man's first-century social involvements, and one is immediately confronted by an emaciated and insipid message, irrelevant to man's critical needs. This is not to make of the Christian message a mere tool for social betterment and community improvement. It is to say, and quite pointedly, that true prophets, then and now, must deal with the festering problems of their own respective generations.

In view of this continuingly valid principle, Amos addressed himself directly to the corruption of his own society. He did not hesitate to confront the leadership of Israel with the enormity of its sin.

Designation of the offenders, 4:1a.—The ultimate cause of corruption was traced directly to the women of the day. In stinging words the prophet called to them saying, "Hear this word, you cows of Bashan." Bashan, east of the Jordan and north of Gilead, was noted for the sleek, well-fed cattle that grazed upon its pastures (cf. Deut. 32:14). The prime offenders in Israel were her women, designated as fat, sleek cattle. George Adam Smith observed: "There is a prophet's insight into character. Not of Jezebels, or Messalinas, or Lady-Macbeths is it spoken, but of the ordinary matrons of Samaria. Thoughtlessness and luxury are able to make brutes out of women of gentle nurture, with homes and a religion."[1]

Description of their offenses, 4:1b.—The women of the day were guilty of oppressing the poor and crushing the needy. Such action was not direct but indirect, yet the women were responsible. It was at their insistent demand that their husbands oppressed others in order to obtain the luxuries of the day. "They say unto their lords [husbands]: 'Bring, that we may drink.'" Described as fat cattle that hooked, pushed, and shoved until the weaker cattle were denied their portions, the women of the day were appropriately identified as those who oppressed the poor and crushed the needy. Their condemnation lay not in that they were fat and sleek, but that in the midst of their plenty the poverty of the masses was to be observed. As Luthi indicates, "that is the uncanny thing, that at all times, even in the leanest of times and on every pasture, even on the driest, there are still fat cattle."[2]

The depression of the 1930s witnessed the destruction of a national economy, but even then there were those who quite aptly could be described as "fat cattle." World War II with its honor rolls of dead and its shortages of foods also had those who emerged the fatter at the expense of the less fortunate. Indeed, Amos' charge is a parable on all of human existence. "The poor are always with us," society is often reminded. Society should be reminded just as often that the fat cattle who have grown sleek at the expense of the poor are also always with us.

Denunciation of the offenders, 4:2-3.—Such action could not escape the notice, evaluation, and judgment of God. That is, it could not

---

[1] *Op. cit.*, I, 150.
[2] *Op. cit.*, p. 52.

escape if one accepted three propositions: (1) the existence of God, (2) the moral nature of God, and (3) the unlimited power of God.

Corrupt action in society was, therefore, denounced by God himself. Indeed, Amos could write on behalf of God,

> The Lord God has sworn by his holiness
>   that, behold, the days are coming upon you,
> when they shall take you away with hooks,
>   even the last of you with fishhooks.
> And you shall go out through the breaches,
>   every one straight before her;
>   and you shall be cast forth into Harmon (4:2-3).

The verb "sworn" could also be translated "he has sworn himself." The verb is a simple passive (Niphal), but one which may at times be translated in a reflexive sense (i.e., the action is by one's self upon one's own person). Such an expression was used of taking an oath (cf. Psalm 15:4) and graphically portrayed the action of God in this case (4:2). God had sworn himself. He had, reflexively, bound himself with an oath. Not by an external power, but in and of himself as an expression of his character he had vowed to act in view of man's corrupt society. Not only did he "swear himself," but he did so "by his holiness." The action of God is grounded in the character of God, his deeds being the expression of what he is.

Such action of God as portrayed by Amos took place in historical processes. The prophet saw the events of history as an expression of God's judgment. For him the correlation between history and God's will was direct. Israel was corrupt and in such a state had sown the seeds of her own destruction. The words of Amos found their fulfilment within the lifetime of many who heard him speak. The exile of 722 B.C. and following was not only the dissolution of the Northern Kingdom. For Amos, it was the judgment of God upon a corrupt society.

In such a time of judgment Amos proclaimed, "They shall take you away with hooks, even the last of you with fishhooks" (4:2). This should be understood literally since it was the Assyrian custom to lead away the more conspicuous captives by a hook passed through the nose or the lip (cf. Isa. 37:29). This custom is reflected in the pictures which may be seen on Assyrian monuments.[3]

---

[3] Gwynn, *op. cit.*, p. 18.

In conclusion, Amos pointed out that the women would go out through the breaches made in the city wall, "a woman before her" (literally), or "each woman straight before her; and you (feminine) shall be cast into Harmon" (4:3). There is little agreement concerning "Harmon." Each of the following should be considered:

1. The Targum, Peshitta, and Vulgate understood it as Armenia.
2. Chajes, the Jewish scholar, ingeniously connected it with the Arabic "harem": their destination is the harems of their captors.[4]
3. The Syrian god Rimmon, to whose service the women are assigned.
4. "Hermon," the mountain region north of Bashan.

Despite the lack of clarity today, the meaning would have been clear in Amos' day and no doubt carried the connotation of extreme misfortune. Beyond this one cannot conscientiously go in seeking to state the meaning intended. Suffice it to say, however, that exile to a most unpleasant situation was envisioned by Amos as judgment upon the people for the corruption of society.

One reads this condemnation of the "first ladies of Samaria" with a note of sadness. But the pathos is multiplied when one considers that the same conditions still prevail. Society is still corrupt when the inordinate demands for luxurious surroundings produce an insensitive attitude to the needs of others. So long as some walk on carpeted floors, while others seek to avoid the splinters in an unfinished, pine floor, the problem remains. So long as modern society can ignore the crying need of men without adequate food, children without clothing, and women condemned to a life of sordid travail —the social system is corrupt. Not only on the mountains of Samaria, but in the valleys of every community the fat cows of Bashan still feed and fatten themselves. They still hook and gore, push and shove, all the while saying, "Bring us more." Nothing is more corrupt than a society insensitive to the needs of its poor and needy.

The Degenerate Ecclesiasticism Represented by a Superficial Formalism, 4:4-5

The second evil, a degenerate ecclesiasticism, was manifested by the superficial formalism in the worship of the day. If surveys had

---

[4] S. M. Lehrman, "Amos," *The Twelve Prophets*, ed. A. Cohen (Bournemouth, Hampshire: The Soncino Press, 1948), p. 98.

been in vogue at that time, they would have revealed a yearly advance in every area of activity. Indeed, it is doubtful if a day would have been left without a special emphasis. People were thronging the sites of worship, tithes were being multiplied beyond budgetary requirements, sacrifices were numerous, and offerings "over and above the tithe" (i.e. the freewill offerings) were flowing freely. Not only was all of this taking place at the sanctuaries, but the people were quite satisfied with such religious veneer. Indeed, proclaimed Amos, "so you love to do, O people of Israel!" (4:5). For the activist, religion was at its apex; for God, religion was at its lowest point.

Herein is to be found the most pressingly relevant problem of contemporary denominational structures. Can religion be outwardly successful and satisfying, yet inwardly degenerate and perverted? Amos said that it could be no more than a degenerate ecclesiasticism overly concerned with the externals.

Sarcastic invitation to worship, 4:4.—"Come to Bethel, and transgress," called the prophet, "to Gilgal, and multiply transgression" (4:4a). Bethel [5] and Gilgal [6] had long been religious centers in Israel and, therefore, were singled out by Amos in his attack upon the superficiality of Israel's worship. The call of the prophet for the people to come to Bethel and to Gilgal is saturated with both irony and sarcasm. As Elijah had done on Mount Carmel (1 Kings 18), Amos also called upon the people to observe their superficial worship.[7]

Not only by this note of sarcasm were the people indicted, but by the content of the invitation as well. The invitation was not "come to worship." Amos called, "Come to Bethel, and *transgress*." The word is from *pāshaʿ* and is identical in background with the word used in the indictments against foreign nations (cf. Amos 1:3, 6,9,11,13, etc.). The word literally means a rebellion. For example, "the king of Moab rebelled against the king of Israel" (2 Kings 3:5). Sin, therefore, is an act of rebellion against constituted authority. It is a volitional act of the will resulting in estrangement from the object of one's rebellion.

---

[5] Cf. Gen. 12:8; 28:11-13,22; 1 Sam. 7:16; 13:2; 1 Kings 12:29,32.

[6] Cf. Hos. 4:15; 9:15; 12:11; Amos 5:5.

[7] Lehrman, *op. cit.*, p. 98.

Worship had so degenerated in the time of Amos that it could be called a rebellion—a *pesha'*, the common word for transgression in the Old Testament. At this juncture Amos would no doubt have given assent to the call of a later prophet, Malachi, who viewed the superficiality and meaninglessness of worship in his time and cried out, "Oh, that there were one among you who would shut the doors, that you might not kindle fire upon my altar in vain! I have no pleasure in you, says the Lord of hosts" (1:10). How tragic and how pathetic it was that religion had become so perverted that a prophet, rather than issuing a call to worship, issued a call for someone to close the doors to the house of God. But worship had become so superficial that the prophet had no other choice.

One wonders what an Amos or a Malachi would do in the presence of current religious structures. While well-intentioned men do their best to lead in a godly manner, it would seem that the burden and the force of secularism are so great as to negate their efforts. Would Amos call to modern man saying, "Come up to your ornate buildings upon which you have lavished the money from your corrupt social system, perform your ritual. Piously endure the rapid staccato of a hurriedly prepared, hastily delivered sermon. Come up to the church at eleven o'clock Sunday morning and *rebel* against God"? Would Malachi cry out in this twentieth century, "Oh, that there were one among you who would shut the doors that you might not worship in vain"?

While such may represent an extreme attitude, it does focus upon a real problem, a suicidal problem. Somehow there must come to modern society another great awakening, the realization that although one may possess all of religion's externals, the inner life may be gone. Unless some such awakening comes we may well go forth as Samson did to meet his foes, saying, "'I will go out as at other times, and shake myself free.' And he did not know that the Lord had left him" (Judg. 16:20). Is it not possible that contemporary ecclesiastical structures are much like Samson? Proud to the point of self-righteous arrogance, they do not consider that despite their previous conquests the Lord may now have left them. This is the haunting threat that every generation must face!

Invitation to offer elaborate and multiplied acts of worship, 4:4b-5a.—The sarcastic call of Amos entreated the people to

> bring your sacrifices every morning,
>> your tithes every three days;
> offer a sacrifice of thanksgiving of that which is leavened,
>> and proclaim freewill offerings, publish them;
> for so you love to do, O people of Israel!

Such elaborate ritual had not been prescribed. Sacrifice was required no more than three times during the year, or even only once.[8] Also, the tithe was demanded only every third year,[9] not every third day. Amos thus called upon Israel to offer on a daily basis that which had been demanded annually. The verse is a sarcastic thrust at the multiplication of ritual reflected in its daily observance.

The same ridicule of Israel's worship can be seen in the prophet's call to "offer a sacrifice of thanksgiving of that which is leavened." The use of leaven was forbidden in both early and late Israelite law.[10] Amos was concerned, however, not with the violation of a cultic law, but attempted by this means to indicate the "mistaken zeal (possibly a survival of Baal-worship) in which the worshippers thought to make their thanksgiving-offering more acceptable."[11]

The superficiality of eighth-century religious forms was further indicated by Amos' call for freewill offerings. Such offerings were voluntary in nature (cf. Ex. 35:29), but in the context of Amos 4:5 were obviously capitalized upon in order to exalt the giver. The degenerate nature of worship could hardly have been made more vivid than through this portrayal of hypocritical, freewill offerings, publicly proclaimed for all to behold.

Motivation for such acts of worship, 4:5b.—All such worship described by Amos (4:4-5) was based upon the assumption that "so you love to do, O people of Israel." While one may accept this as sincere and adequate motivation, in view of the total context it would seem that this was actually a quite superficial attitude. One may, indeed, love to perform acts of worship without being either hypocritical or insincere. In fact, worship of a true nature is predicated upon a love for God as expressed in worship. Worship becomes degenerate, however, when it is loved in and of itself. One may well

---

[8] Cripps, *op. cit.*, p. 170.
[9] Cf. Deut. 14:28; 26:12.
[10] Cf. Lev. 2:11; 6:17; Ex. 23:18.
[11] Cripps, *op. cit.*, pp. 170-71.

become so enmeshed in the ritual of worship that he never beholds the object of worship. In essence, worship can become the object of veneration rather than God. Israel did love the ritual, but in exalting it they had obscured God.

Making worship an end in itself rather than a means to an end is a problem of the twentieth century A.D. even as it was for the eighth century B.C. The end in view should always be the adoration and exaltation of God through worship. In a day when so much emphasis is placed upon technique and procedure one may succumb to the error of deifying the system and worshiping the created rather than the creator. Of true worship, every man should have it said, "for so you love to do." At the same time, one should be quite cautious lest he begin to love only the form and forget the content of true worship.

Marks of a degenerate ecclesiasticism.—When may it be said of any ecclesiastical or denominational structure, of any day, that it has grown degenerate and corrupt? It could be said that this condition exists whenever it is characterized by the following points of similarity with those of Amos' day.

First, ecclesiastical structures are degenerate and corrupt when quantity is substituted for quality. The relevant issue is not how many altars or how many sacrifices, but what is offered at the altar and what spirit accompanies the sacrifice. The point of significance is not "how many" but "how much." As someone has observed concerning contemporary church members: "It's time we stopped counting them and started weighing them."

Second, ecclesiasticism is degenerate when it can substitute form for content, externalities for spiritual realities, and be satisfied with both of these.

Third, ecclesiasticism is corrupt when it can substitute the ritual of sacrifice, tithes, and freewill offerings for an experiential encounter with the God of forgiveness. In far too many cases such externals are but substitutes for genuine religious encounter, and are used by a guilty people to ease a troubled conscience. A contemporary writer has expressed it well.

I tremble lest these countless "free offerings" are coming more and more to have the significance the peasant from Tekoa saw in the offerings at Beth-el and Gilgal. Let the Christian Church be sure, when she calls to sacrifice, that she does it in a Christian way! Let her make sure that "free offerings" do not merely serve to strengthen contentment with half measures, lukewarmness, and mediocrity! Let her be certain that our free offering does not become a pretext for making our sojourn on a bed of ease more tolerable by means of a cheap commutation for sin![12]

Fourth, ecclesiasticism has become degenerate and corrupt when it is an end in itself, obscuring the reality of divine communion. Israel could cry, "for so we love to do!" Yet, the Israel of Amos' day did not know God. Indeed, a prophet of the same generation could say, "My people are destroyed for lack of knowledge" (Hos. 4:6). The same prophet talked of the futility of superficial worship as he spoke for God, saying,

> With their flocks and herds they shall go
>   to seek the Lord,
> but they will not find him;
>   he has withdrawn from them (Hos. 5:6).

No one knows how many go with all sincerity, today, to seek God but cannot find him in the maze of a twentieth-century, mass-produced program of worship. How many attend worship services seeking God, but go away saying, as one college professor said: "Sometimes I come away and wonder why I ever went!" At times it is the fault of the individual. Yet, how many times has it been the fault of an ecclesiasticism out of touch with the needs of twentieth-century man? How many have come asking bread, only to receive a stone? How many have asked for a fish, but received a serpent? An ecclesiastical structure that has displaced God will be displaced by God. In fact, such displacement of God is self-destructive, carrying within itself the seeds of its own annihilation.

Israel's Failure to Return, 4:6-11

The primary function of the Israelite prophet was that of relating the events of history to the will of God. Amos, for example, saw on the one hand the corruption of Israelite society and the degenerate ecclesiasticism of the day. On the other hand, he witnessed the crises of history which brought terror to the land. Drought,

---

[12] Luthi, *op. cit.*, p. 57.

famine, plague, war, and earthquake brought the prophet and his contemporaries face to face with realities of unspeakable horror. What was the relationship between social and ecclesiastical evils of the day and current disastrous events? In the mind of Amos there was but one answer. Such catastrophes were the judgment of God upon the sins of Israel. The validity of such an assumption for twentieth-century Christendom will be discussed later in the development of this chapter. Suffice it to say that for Amos there was no question concerning the validity of equating such catastrophes with the judgment of God. In his mind these events constituted God's method of redemptive judgment, redemptive in that it sought to bring Israel back to God.

In seeking to relate the catastrophic events of his generation to the will of God, Amos (1) cited the various catastrophes, and (2) indicated the failure of Israel to respond to the judgment of God.

Redemptive Judgment That Should Have Brought Repentance

Amos isolated five separate, yet closely related, catastrophes that should have caused Israel to turn toward God. The underlying assumption of the prophet centered in the fact that judgment in history has a redemptive purpose. It is intended to cause man to see his desperate need for God, and subsequently to turn to his fellowship and communion. It should be emphasized, of course, that such redemptive value is true only of judgment in history. Man's relationship with God is fixed at death (cf. Luke 16:19-31) and cannot thereafter be altered. In the framework of history, however, judgment is with redemptive purpose. The judgment of God is not like that of a man whose action is solely retributive, with little or no thought of restitution. The catastrophes of Amos 4:6-11 should be viewed against the concept of judgment with redemptive purpose.

Starvation was a haunting reality for the land. "I gave you cleanness of teeth in all your cities, and lack of bread in all your places," said Amos as he spoke for God (4:6). In a section of synonymous parallelism the prophet sought to emphasize the calamity produced by famine. The meaning of "cleanness of teeth" should be obvious; they were clean because the people possessed no food to cling to the teeth.

The significant emphasis made by the prophet was that such

famine had been sent by God. "I gave you cleanness of teeth." In the mind of Amos the famine was the result of God's activity. The action of God is intensified by a literal translation of the Hebrew text: "And also I, I gave you cleanness of teeth." The personal pronoun is contained within the verb and the addition of the separate pronoun to the verbal construction is for the purpose of emphasis. The prophet added the separate pronoun since he wanted to leave no doubt that the famine was brought about by God.

In view of the biblical emphasis upon the value of human personality, how is one to reconcile the question of famine with the will of God? Especially is this relevant when, as in this case, the innocent suffer with the guilty. The use of the word "reconcile" is perhaps too optimistic, for there is no absolute answer to the problem. One can, however, seek to understand how an Old Testament prophet could attribute calamities, such as the five in Amos 4:6-11, to the direct action of God. Briefly, such an attitude arose from two considerations.

First, the moral problem was not as relevant to the thought pattern of that day as it was after the appearance of Jesus and his higher revelation. Today, no one would seriously seek to maintain the equality of the morality found in the Old Testament with that of the New Testament. As a result it should be recognized that the Old Testament personality was completely untroubled by many of the moral problems that confront the Christian.

Second, the ancient Hebrew did not distinguish between natural law and divine action. The Hebrew vocabulary had no word for "nature." Where the modern man would use the word "nature," the Hebrew would in almost all instances have used "God." Consequently, the Hebrew did not deal with secondary causes. Such simply did not exist for the ancient mind. If anything happened, "God did it" (cf. 3:3-8). These two emphases do not explain why the prophet thought as he did. But they should, however, make it easier to understand how he could hold such a position.

To the starvation that ravaged the country, Amos added drought, an attendant and, perhaps, a causative disaster (4:7-8). The interpretation of drought as judgment is strengthened by the consideration of two of its characteristics. First, it came at a most inopportune time. "I also withheld the rain from you when there were yet three months to the harvest," said Amos (4:7). The rain was withheld at a time when the soil needed it most. The timing of the event made it even more catastrophic than ever.

Second, the drought was not universal. Had it fallen upon everyone it might have been the more easily dismissed. Since it rained upon one city but not upon another, upon one field but not the other, the interpretation of the event as an act of judgment was easier. The very fact that the drought came with such a high degree of discrimination was indicative of its judgmental nature; some were singled out, some were spared.

As if drought had not been catastrophic enough, disease and insect were added to bring about the destruction of the crops.

> "I smote you with blight and mildew;
>   I laid waste your gardens and your vineyards;
>   your fig trees and your olive trees the locust devoured;
> yet you did not return to me,"
>   says the Lord (4:9).

In all probability, the blight and the mildew were caused, respectively, by the hot east wind (the sirocco) and the dampness of late autumn.[13] Evidently this attack was at a different time than the drought, since mildew would require moisture before it could take place. Such an attack laid waste the vineyards and the gardens, while locusts devoured the fig trees and the olive trees. The picture was one of absolute devastation. The drought three months prior to harvest time had taken its toll, while the blight and mildew during the autumn rains had added to the destruction. Finally, locusts had devoured the products of the fig trees and the olive trees, bringing to a climax the destruction of the nation's food supplies.

The horror of battle also had come upon Israel. As Amos said,

> "I sent among you a pestilence after the manner of Egypt;
>   I slew your young men with the sword;
> I carried away your horses;
>   and I made the stench of your camp go up into your nostrils;
> yet you did not return to me,"
>   says the Lord (4:10).

---

[13] Lehrman, *op. cit.*, p. 100.

The context of such warfare as described herein must be sought prior to the time of Amos since his was an era of relative peace. Therefore, Amos quite likely had in mind the conflicts of Israel with Syria during the ninth and early eighth centuries. The memory of such periods of devastation were no doubt long remembered and would have served to reflect the judgment of God.

The reference by Amos to the fact that "I overthrew some of you, as when God overthrew Sodom and Gomorrah, and you were as a brand plucked out of the burning" (4:11), should be understood as a reference to the earthquake mentioned in the preface to the book itself (cf. 1:1).[14] Bare escape from such a terrible experience served as adequate evidence for deliverance by God from the depth of such a catastrophe.

Reproaching Refrain

Five times the account of judgment is portrayed. Five times, once at the conclusion of each section, the haunting refrain is heard, "'Yet you did not return to me,' says the Lord" (4:6,8-11). Judgment came but man did not return to God as a result of having experienced disaster and catastrophe.

In view of this, there should have been no doubt but that God's purpose in judgment was redemptive. It was his purpose that judgment should lead to a return by the people. Such was not the case, however, for Israel did not return! In the use of these disasters as a form of judgment, one is confronted with the most important aspect of the entire problem of God's will and natural calamity. The most significant point to consider is not the ultimate or secondary source, a full explanation of the justice of such deeds, or even an attempt to exonerate God. The most important consideration is that of man's response to such catastrophe.

Do acts of this kind lead to a new awareness of God's sovereignty? Do they result in a new committal on the part of man to God? This is the significant element.

A hurricane or a tornado is not necessarily the expression of judgment. All suffering should not be attributed to God, especially in the light of the book of Job. At the same time, catastrophe may well cause man to recognize his finitude in the face of an over-

---

[14] Cripps, *op. cit.*, p. 175.

whelming disaster, thereby opening the way for communion with God. There are few today who would equate every phenomenon of nature with the intentional will of God. Few would see God as directly, morally responsible for the death of a child by an automobile or disease. Many would, however, correctly testify that such crises have underscored their own limitations and helplessness, thereby making it possible to experience new depths of communion with God in such a time of crisis.

The correlation of the events of history and the will of God will never be perfect until man has perfect knowledge of the nature of God. So long as God is God and man is man this will not be attained, since imperfect apprehension is a part of the line of demarcation between God and man. In the meantime, let all men know that the point of emphasis should be placed ultimately, not upon reason, but upon response. As Amos did, so must modern man consider as of primary significance the nature of his response to catastrophe. The moral reason behind such events, while important, must be secondary. We cannot explain them perfectly but we can act in the light of them.

In view of this, history should serve to make man aware of his own dependence. Catastrophe should draw man near to the heart of God in an ever deepening communion. May it never be said that the catastrophes of history failed to draw this generation nearer to God. May it never be said, "Yet you did not return to me."

When All Else Fails: Judgment Must Fall, 4:12-13

When all else has failed, judgment of an unprecedented nature must fall. The turbulent "natural" events in history bear sufficient witness to man's finitude as to lead him to repentance. When such events have failed, however, and man has not returned, the inevitability of unprecedented judgment must realistically be considered.

Preparation Must Be Made, 4:12

Since man had not returned to God, Amos proclaimed, "Therefore thus I will do to you, O Israel; because I will do this to you, prepare to meet your God, O Israel!" (4:12). Indefinite, yet certain judgment awaited such rebellion as that portrayed by the prophet. The threat of judgment itself was indefinite, as elsewhere in the Old Testament—"may the Lord do so to me and more also," (Ruth

1:17). The vagueness may have been deliberate for one of two reasons. The fate was either too terrible to describe, or it was deliberately left quite vague in order to be broad enough to convey any type of judgment imaginable, thus intensifying its sense of dread.

In this warning the prophet made at least three assumptions: (1) men are unprepared to meet God, (2) men must prepare for an inevitable meeting, and (3) men can prepare. At the same time it should be emphasized that the preparation Amos had in mind was not with the idea of escaping God's judgment. Rather, it had the idea of preparation for the terror of judgment which could not be avoided.

Power for Punishment, 4:13

Power for the punishment of Israel was present in the personality of God. Amos expressed this by saying:

> For lo, he who forms the mountains, and creates the wind,
>   and declares to man what is his thought;
> who makes the morning darkness,
>   and treads on the heights of the earth—
> the Lord, the God of hosts, is his name (4:13)!

The power of God was adequate for the task. Such power could be seen in a number of divine characteristics. For example, the creative activity of God testified to the adequacy of his power. "He who forms the mountains, and creates the winds" was surely able to deal with man's rebellion. The mountains and the wind, always two wonders for the Hebrew, represented the height of God's creative power. The action of God thus revealed was continuous (Amos used two participles, yōtsēr and borē') and, therefore, always available.

The power of God was further reflected in revelation. God made known (a participle, used quite often to indicate continuous action) to man his own thoughts: "and declaring to man what is his thought" (4:13). Such self-knowledge could not be attained by man alone (cf. Jer. 17:10). It could be given only by God. Thus, it became a sign of sovereign power.

The turning of morning into darkness was another manifestation of God's power. The turning of evening into darkness was normal, but darkness in the morning was an unusual manifestation of divine power. Amos was quite likely speaking with the eclipse of 763 B.C. as the specific act in mind.

God also "treads on the heights of the earth," said Amos. The earthquake of Amos 1:1 probably produced such a figure of speech as that used here by the prophet. For ancient man, without a geological explanation, an earthquake no doubt did appear as though God himself was treading upon the mountains.

Finally, the name of God was a conclusive evidence of his power. In the Old Testament a name was more than a means of identification. It was the summation of one's life and character. It represented all that a man was. Hence, Isaiah could speak of Immanuel as one who would be literally "God with us" (Isa. 7:14), since such a name expressed the nature, character, and function of the messianic person. With this in the background it is extremely significant that God was spoken of as "Yahweh," and "God of hosts, or armies." The name "Yahweh" was the most personal name of God in all of the Old Testament and was used essentially in the context of the covenant relationship. It was as one to whom Israel was responsible in the covenant that God came in judgment. In addition to this, he was the "God of hosts" (or armies). The figure of God as one who came in charge of an army added to the concept of his power.

In each of these five areas Amos stressed the fact that power adequate for the punishment of Israel was present in the personality of God.

As chapter 4 is viewed in retrospect one would agree that

the true view of the relation of all material things and events to God is this which the herdsman of Tekoa proclaimed. These messengers were not "miracles," but they were God's messengers all the same. Behind all phenomena stands a personal will, and they are nearer the secret of the universe who see God working in it all, than they who see all forces except the One which is the only true force.[15]

---

[15] Maclaren, *op. cit.*, p. 153.

6

When Justice Rolls Down
Like Water

Amos 5:1-27

Irresponsible conduct, whether within or without the religious structures of the day, cannot continue unabated without experiencing inevitable retribution. If man will not hear the word of God in judgment, it is only left for him to experience that judgment in history. This was the disturbing proclamation of the prophet Amos. With a heart that loved Israel deeply (although this is not often emphasized),[1] the prophet stressed that the nation's only hope lay in seeking God. As a consequence of this communion she must let "justice roll down like waters." Only when justice and righteousness roll down in this fashion is there hope either for the individual or for his religious institutions. In a moving appeal Amos sought to impress upon his people the fatal result of forsaking the father (5:1-3), the false concepts of religion that lead one to forsake God (5:4-20), and the failure of superficial religious form to meet the needs of the heart (5:21-27).

Fatal Result of Forsaking the Father, 5:1-3

Man cannot forsake God with impunity. Amos believed that to forsake God involved certain dire consequences for the nation as well as for the individual.

Destruction of the nation, 5:1-2.—Failure to respond to the entreaties proclaimed in chapter 4 meant that the nation would be destroyed. Amos was convinced that Israel was dead. The people did not know it. No one had proclaimed the news, nor had they

---

[1] Cf. the deep concern of Amos for Israel in her great crises, 7:1 ff.

93

sent for the professional mourners; but Israel was dead. It would be hard to say when she died, but she was dead by the time of Amos. She continued to thrive, however, and it was forty years after Amos' time before national extinction came. Yet, for all practical purposes, she was dead. Her death was so certain that Amos could take up the lamentation, used in mourning the dead, over her: "Hear this word which I take up over you in lamentation, O house of Israel: 'Fallen, no more to rise, is the virgin Israel; forsaken on her land, with none to raise her up'" (5:1-2). For the first time, a prophet emphasized that the nation, not simply individuals within it, would be destroyed. Amos could refer to Israel as "the virgin Israel" since she had been unspoiled by total foreign domination prior to the eighth century. But the prophet was convinced that Israel was now dead. Nothing was left except to take up a lamentation of mourning for her violation and her death.

Is this true of modern America? Could this be true of many current denominational institutions? Is it only extreme pessimism to say, "America is dead; this denomination is dead"? The nation is sick; religion is sick. Is there no hope? "Is there no balm in Gilead? Is there no physician there? Why then has the health of the daughter of my people not been restored?" (Jer. 8:22).

Perhaps it is not yet too late. Perhaps we are not yet dead. Perhaps there is yet, at least, a feeble throb of the pulsebeat. If there is, then in the name of the Father let this bit of life be nourished and caused to live again, for to forsake the Father continually will bring inevitable death.

Desolation worked by destructive judgment, 5:3.—Warfare, then as today, constituted the greatest physical threat which the ancient man faced. Drought and famine were severe and brought death and suffering to all, but they did not compare with the havoc brought by war. In clearly understood terms, the prophet described the destruction which would come upon Israel in a time of warfare, a crisis interpreted by the prophets of the Old Testament as God's judgment. Amos said that the time would come when "the city that went forth a thousand shall have a hundred left, and that which went forth a hundred shall have ten left to the house of Israel" (5:3). Not every war of history can be explained as the judgment of God. However, God can make use of such tragedies in the fulfilment of his ultimate will.

False Concepts of Religion Which Led to the Forsaking of God,
5:4-20

It is often difficult to determine whether a specific deed is itself the cause of a subsequent action, or whether it should be viewed primarily as the effect of a preceding cause. This is true in the case of Amos 5:4-20. Did these false concepts lead to the forsaking of God, or did the forsaking of God lead men to adopt these false concepts? It is recognized that valid arguments could be constructed on both sides. The position taken here is that the concepts described are actually principles inherent in the forsaking of God.

The concept that God can be localized and discovered in tradition and ritual, 5:4-9.—Man finds life only as he seeks and finds God. "Seek me and live," Amos called to the people of Israel. The fact that life is found in God is not the point of consideration that brings the greatest difficulty to man. Almost all who believe recognize that life is in God. The continuing problem of man is the rampant confusion on how to find God. In Israel God had become identified with the traditions and rituals of the past. This was not just a problem of Amos' day. Throughout the prophetic era the prophets continually fought against the idea that God could be identified with the ritual and traditions of the ancient places and ways of worship (cf. Hos. 5:1 ff.; Isa. 1:12 ff.; Jer. 7:1 ff.; Ezek. 40 to 48, wherein the entire religious structure was viewed as restored along different lines from the traditional).

Man does not always find God in the traditional and honored means. Therefore, "Seek me and live; but do not seek Bethel, and do not enter into Gilgal or cross over to Beer-sheba," called the Lord through the prophet (5:4-5). Because man does not always find God in the traditional and accepted patterns, Amos contrasted seeking God, on the one hand, with going up to the primary religious centers of Israel, on the other. Men may have gone to Bethel, Gilgal, and Beer-sheba, but God would not meet them there.

The old ways are not to be forsaken simply because of their antiquity, however, for in most instances they contain the way to God. At the same time, antiquity does not validate the way. God will not be found, even though men throng the places of worship, so long as they "turn justice to wormwood, and cast down righteousness to the earth!" (5:7). A way is valid only if it meets the test of divine confirmation through the total revelation of God, not through just a part of the revelation. Tradition is not necessarily to be equated with God.

God is too great to be encompassed by the boundaries of traditionalism and ritual. Amos expressed this by saying:

> He who made the Pleiades and Orion,
>   and turns deep darkness into the morning,
>   and darkens the day into night,
> who calls for the waters of the sea,
>   and pours them out upon the surface of the earth,
> the Lord is his name,
> who makes destruction flash forth against the strong,
>   so that destruction comes upon the fortress (5:8-9).

The very descriptive image of God presented here is too large to be encompassed by human forms and altars, whether it be Bethel, Gilgal, or some other local center. A god like this cannot be confined by any neat package prepared by man. How egotistical it is, therefore, that man becomes so disturbed in not being able to understand the nature of God completely. In his pride, man does not recognize that a "god" who could be localized and defined in precise human terms would not be God at all.

At the precise moment at which man can comprehend every detail of the divine nature, at that very moment God will have ceased to be God and man will have become God. Amos insisted that God could not be localized, for he threw the stars into their orbits; he made the Pleiades and Orion. The dawning of every day was a new revelation of the magnitude of God as he turned night into day, and in turn darkened day into night (5:8a). Every rain was a refreshing reminder that God was too big to be confined at Bethel.

As one writer has indicated concerning the conception of God held by many, "your God is too small."[2] This was the heart of Israel's error. God is too big to be confined at Bethel, localized at Gilgal, or identified with Jerusalem. This is a disturbing proclamation, especially if the one who hears or reads it is identified with Bethel, Gilgal, or some other geographical site of institutionalized religion.

---

[2] J. B. Phillips, *Your God Is Too Small* (New York: The Macmillan Co., 1956).

You cannot identify God with a geographical spot on earth any more than you can equate him with the sum total of an organization. God is too big for this. He may include all of this, but he is always more; he always goes beyond this. The sin of Israel was that of formulating the concept of a "little god," one who could be localized and identified with man's own attempt to express his faith.

The concept that human personality could be abused for personal gain, without divine retribution, 5:10-13.—The second concept that led to the breaking of divine fellowship was the idea that human personality could be abused without divine retribution. Nothing could ever have been farther removed from the will of God. Yet, this characterized the thought of many in the time of Amos (cf. 2:6 ff.; 6:1 ff.; 8:4 ff.). The fact that all men are made in the image of God demands equal respect for the personality of every man. It was upon this principle that biblical reverence for life was established. "Whoever sheds the blood of man, by man shall his blood be shed; for God made man in his own image" (Gen. 9:6).

No man made in the image of God can be abused without divine judgment. This finds confirmation in the testimony of Jesus Christ: "Truly, I say to you, as you did it to one of the least of these my brethren, you did it to me" (Matt. 25:40). Here is the very foundation for the equal treatment of every man regardless of race, color, or creed: man bears in him the image of God, and what one does to man is also done to God. As do many today, Israel may have known this theoretically. But she practiced it with no more practicality than does contemporary society.

Caught up in an era of disregard for human personality, Amos' generation rejected any corrective word addressed to it. The leaders of the Israelite community often gathered about the city gate, much as small towns today have their places of assembly (cf. Ruth 4:1; Job 29:7 ff.; Prov. 31:23 ff.). When men, probably prophets, appeared "in the gate" with a corrective word for the people, they could not gain a hearing. In fact, "They hate him who reproves in the gate, and they abhor him who speaks the truth" (5:10).

People have not changed greatly. No one likes to hear a word of correction; even though it may be uttered by those as concerned or more concerned for the corporate good as any individual within the group. Men are still like Ahab who said, "There is yet one man by whom we may inquire of the Lord, Micaiah the son of Imlah; but I hate him, for he never prophesies good concerning me, but evil" (1 Kings 22:8). God did not call his prophets, ancient or modern, to proclaim a soothing word of consolation but to proclaim the will of God as the prophet came to see that will. To be sure the word was proclaimed with a sympathetic heart as in the case of Hosea. At times God did not allow its proclamation until the prophet had gone "to sit where the people sit" (Ezek. 3:15-16). Yet, when a prophet could speak in love, and when he had sat where the people were, he had the responsibility of speaking the full counsel of God. Thus, every modern prophet must also proclaim the revelation of God, despite the nature of its severity. When this is done men do not want to hear!

Human personality had been abused in many varied ways in eighth-century Israel. Primary among these, in the mind of Amos, were the elaborate buildings and the accumulated lands that had been amassed by the wealthy. The sin of Israel lay in the fact that much of this had been accumulated at the expense of the poor.

> Therefore because you trample upon the poor
>   and take from him exactions of wheat,
> you have built houses of hewn stone,
>   but you shall not dwell in them;
> you have planted pleasant vineyards,
>   but you shall not drink their wine.
> For I know how many are your transgressions,
>   and how great are your sins—
> you who afflict the righteous, who take a bribe,
>   and turn aside the needy in the gate (5:11-12).

The poor man, trampled upon by the powerful, gave his exaction of wheat and paid for the extravagant indulgencies of the rich. The righteous had been afflicted by men who took a bribe and testified against them, as in the false accusation made against Naboth a century earlier (cf. 1 Kings 21:1 ff.). The needy had been turned aside at the gate because of the lack of concern for the less fortunate that characterized the powerful in Israel. Because of this abuse of human personality, the powerful classes in Israel's society had been able to build the very best for themselves. Not content with erecting houses of common "field stone," they had utilized the more expensive "hewn stone," quarried and shaped by underpaid, oppressed workmen. They planted pleasant vineyards, as Ahab had his herb garden before them. All of this they did through the blood and sweat of the oppressed. Little wonder that the blood of the innocent cried out from the wall against them (cf. Hab. 2:11), as the blood of Abel had cried from the ground against his brother (cf. Gen. 4:10).

Expressed in twentieth-century terms, they had their rambling houses sprawled over elaborate lots, their carpeted floors, two- and three-car garages, paved patios, and well-filled freezers. All of this is yours, a modern Amos would say, because of your trampling of the weak. The modern world possesses millions who have never known a full meal in the North American sense, and who go to bed hungry every night. Yet, America must consider the problem of excess food that cannot be eaten, and surplus fabrics that cannot be worn. Half the world earns less than one hundred dollars per year; yet, the modern American still does not recognize the reason for turmoil in South America, Africa, or the Far East!

Can this continue? Amos said that it could not. He emphasized that God knows of this and with this knowledge shall act in judgment. "For I know," says the Lord (5:12).

Some men may never know the reality of suffering because of their failure to take time to consider it as a real problem. Others do not know of it because they have forced themselves to ignore it, not wanting to be troubled with "the other fellow's problem." Humanity can be sure of this: God knows it, and in the long stretch of history will act to bring it to an end. A society built on injustice and fed on the sufferings of the underprivileged can never stand.

In all turbulent times there is always the advice, "he who is prudent will keep silent in such a time; for it is an evil time" (5:13). Cripps suggests that these words are perhaps a later, apocalyptic gloss as a word of warning to the hearer or reader.[3] It does seem that they are not the words of Amos, or, if written or spoken by him, they should be understood as Amos' quotation of a common proverb of the day. The situation had so deteriorated that the "smart" man would keep quiet. The same situation prevails in every generation. It may concern political corruption or racial tension.

---

[3] *Op. cit.*, pp. 188-89.

It even drifts into the church and denominational life. Luthi says,

Keep silence! Cringe! Keep your mouth shut! For God's sake don't be-
tray even by an eyelash, even by a wrinkle on your brow, what you feel
inside! . . . Many a one has his wife or mother call after him implor-
ingly as he leaves the house every day: "For heaven's sake don't get
carried away! Put up with it! Be prudent! Keep silence!" Therefore the
prudent shall keep silence in that time; for it is an evil time.[4]

There is one who will not keep silent. God will not keep silent,
for he yet speaks through the Scriptures. He will continue to speak
if voices will rise up in this generation to become true prophets such
as was Amos. Human personality cannot be abused for personal gain
without divine retribution. This generation would do well to accept
the validity of this by the hearing of the ear rather than to wait and
know it by the breaking of the life.

The concept that religion and morality are separate, 5:14-17.—
The abuse of human personality actually stems from the concept that
religion and morality are separate. This explains, in part, why a
seemingly religious people can be guilty of the gross abuse of
human personality. Man has never identified religion and morality
as fully as they should have been united, thus allowing certain
abuses to take place as a result.

This was the common view of the day: religion and morality are
separate. While some cultures in Israel's background associated
religion and morality,[5] there was never the vital association demanded by the faith of Israel. Especially was this true of Canaanite
religion, and even the people of Israel in Amos' day felt that they
could oppress and then find forgiveness by going to the Temple,
making offerings, and observing other ritual commandments.[6] Quite
likely the people were sincere enough in going up to the Temple.
No doubt some realized that God wanted more than the sweet sa-
vour of the sacrifice and the bodily presence of man at the sanctuary.
"Offer right sacrifices, and put your trust in the Lord" (Psalm 4:5).
The error of Israel lay in that they just did not see the connection

---

[4] *Op. cit.,* p. 74. This contemporary European preacher speaks out of personal acquaintance with twenty years of oppression.

[5] E.g., The Code of Hammurabi ascribes its origin to Shamash, the sun-god.
Egypt, also, had high moral standards.

[6] Cf. the later denunciation of this in Jer. 7:1 ff.

between religion and morality. Amos made two relevant observations concerning this.

First, the prophet insisted that religion must be united with morality. He felt this with such fervor that he could identify seeking God with seeking good. In verse 4 he said, "Seek me and live." In verse 14 he said, "Seek good, and not evil, that you may live." In the mind of the prophet, God and good were irrevocably united with one another. The call to all humanity is:

> Seek good, and not evil,
>   that you may live;
> and so the Lord, the God of hosts, will be with you,
>   as you have said.
> Hate evil, and love good,
>   and establish justice in the gate;
> it may be that the Lord, the God of hosts,
>   will be gracious to the remnant of Joseph (5:14-15).

Amos avoided a serious error, however, for he did not substitute morality for religion, but made religion the basis of morality. Calkins observes, "he taught that all morality finds its roots, its spiritual source and its compelling power over the consciences of men in the character of God Himself, that is, in religion."[7] Many social reformers have never made this distinction.

Elton Trueblood has very incisively pointed out that America has produced a cut-flower civilization. He describes the great principles of social justice, the democratic ideal, and other primary values as derived from the Judeo-Christian religion. These religious roots have been cut, however, and we are attempting to maintain an ethic without a religion. This is America's cut-flower civilization. Cut flowers are beautiful to behold, but inevitably they wither and die because their roots have been severed. Because of this, Trueblood, insists, the American way of life has produced an ethic without a religion, while the chaotic powers of the world have a religion without an ethic.[8] For Amos, this was the heart of irreligion, since "the religion of Israel had become a religion for the rich, the priest and the nobles were linking together in unrighteousness, and the most

---

[7] *Op. cit.*, p. 30.
[8] *The Predicament of Modern Man* (New York: Harper & Bros., 1944), pp. 47-66.

flagrant scenes of immorality and oppression were seen at the sacred courts."[9]

The solution to the problem lay, quite significantly, not in a revolution but in a reformation. The prophets were not innovators but reformers—men who sought to call the nation back to the ideals of former religious experiences, especially from the time of Moses and forward. They insisted that life must be lived in conformity with the covenant. This continues as a valid principle. The Western world does not need a revolution, it needs a reformation. T. H. Robinson suggests that

the Nazarite and the Rechabite . . . had one cure for the diseases of Israel, Amos had another. To them the evil was civilisation, and was to be cured only by the most drastic social surgery. . . . The difficulties could be met only by abolishing the whole scheme of life as practised by Samaria.[10]

Such a position, he continues, "was only natural to an honest, enthusiastic, but shortsighted man. It is inevitable that fresh conditions of life should bring with them fresh possibilities of evil."[11] The position of Amos, on the other hand, was not one of denouncing the system as such, but in working out the principles already learned from God on the desert. There was nothing wrong with life in Canaan that could not be cured by a return to the reality of Israel's earlier divine communion. In this Amos proved to be the wiser and left for all succeeding generations a productive solution to social ills. That is, if each generation will but be willing to walk with courage the path of a Moses, an Amos, a Jeremiah, or a Jesus of Nazareth.

Second, the prophet insisted that religion must be destroyed if it is not united with morality. Having pointed out the solution to the social problems of the day, Amos injected a further warning.

> "In all the squares there shall be wailing;
>   and in all the streets they shall say, 'Alas! alas!'
> They shall call the farmers to mourning

---

[9] W. R. Smith, *op. cit.*, p. 139.

[10] *Prophecy and the Prophets in Ancient Israel* (New York: Charles Scribner's Sons, 1923), p. 67.

[11] *Ibid.*

> and to wailing those who are skilled in lamentation,
> and in all vineyards there shall be wailing,
> for I will pass through the midst of you,"
> says the Lord (5:16-17).

Unless the sin of Israel was corrected, national destruction would be inevitable. Amos saw a time when even the farmers would be called to join those skilled in lamentation, the professional mourners of the day whose lamentation constituted a part of the Israelite funeral. Having known the higher way of religion being joined with morality, and having denied that union, Israel could only face destruction. As one writer has suggested: "No consideration, political or religious, must be suffered to dam the stream of righteousness. Spiritual worship, purity of life, and above all, justice, must be established and maintained as the indispensable conditions of a safe and happy future." [12]

The prophets had no specific proposals to make for the social reorientation of the nation, except a change in the individual within the nation. The aim of Amos was that of uniting religion and morality. Once this was done on an experiential basis, the problem would take care of itself. Society will never be changed except as men are changed. The only power sufficient to transform man is to be found in the incarnation of God in Jesus Christ who alone can lead man willingly to the point of self-crucifixion.

The concept that men will be judged on the basis of external relationships, 5:18-20.—The faith of Israel, as practically every religion, looked forward to a future time of judgment upon the evil forces of the world, judgment accompanied by the vindication and exaltation of the righteous. In Israel this expressed itself in the concept of the "day of the Lord." Originating initially, in all probability, with the concept of a day of battle, the "day of the Lord" came to express the eschatological hopes of the nation.

As is far too often the case, Israel perverted this concept by viewing it primarily as a time for the exaltation of God's people and the judgment of her enemies, with no thought of the judgment of Israel herself. This oversimplification constituted one of the greatest threats to the nation in the time of Amos. People had come to feel

---

[12] Oesterley and Robinson, *op. cit.*, p. 368.

that because they were the chosen of God, all would be well for them in the "day of the Lord." This exclusiveness saturated the Old Testament and manifested itself also in the days of Jesus' ministry. John the Baptist (Matt. 3:9) dealt with the same spirit and chastised the Israel of his day, saying, "Do not presume to say to yourselves, 'We have Abraham as our father'; for I tell you, God is able from these stones to raise up children to Abraham."

The desire for the day of the Lord was widely held, because it was felt to be the time of national deliverance. The truth of the matter was that it would be a time of national deliverance, but deliverance only of the remnant that constituted the true Israel. It is quite often the element of truth present in a concept that makes it the easier to confuse the truth or error of the total idea. Israel failed to see that although the day of the Lord would be a time of national deliverance, it would also be a time of national judgment. Having known oppression during practically all of her existence, it was only logical that Israel should have longed for a time of deliverance. No doubt, people fervently spoke of the way in which life would be vindicated, once the day of the Lord was manifested.

To those with such a superficial concept of the day of God's deliverance, Amos could say, "Woe to you who desire the day of the Lord!" The description of the true nature of the day of the Lord given by Amos was in no way like the common expectation. It was a day of "darkness, and not light. . . . Is not the day of the Lord darkness, and not light, and gloom with no brightness in it?" (5:18b, 20). Indeed the day of the Lord would be, "as if a man fled from a lion, and a bear met him; or went into the house and leaned with his hand against the wall, and a serpent bit him" (5:19).

If the context were not so serious, the predicament of the man described by Amos would have been humorous. Out of one crisis into another, the poor man could never find freedom from danger and destruction. Having escaped from the lion, he immediately met a bear. Then, rushing into the house he breathlessly threw one hand upon the wall for support as he caught his breath, only to have his hand bitten by a serpent. The day of the Lord was to be such a time as this, insisted Amos. It would be a time of inescapable crisis, a time of inevitable judgment, a time when man would be abandoned by every known source of aid.

Has not every individual and every generation been guilty of reliance upon superficial concepts and ideas, even as the generation to which Amos addressed himself? One wonders when he hears some speak of the longing with which they anticipate the return of Christ if they are not in much the same position as those of Amos' day. When the superficiality of the modern church and its ministries are considered, when the abandoned opportunities have been called to testify, one wonders if that time will not be for many, even within the framework of Christendom, a time of "gloom and no brightness in it." When the "books" are examined and every man judged in the light of the deeds of this life (Rev. 20:12), will it be darkness or light? Where then will be the physical programs that we activists have spawned? Where then will be the superiority now felt by many?

It is not easy to distinguish between the essential and the non-essential, the outer form and the inner content. No man would knowingly follow the nonessential or the mere form of religion if he could make the proper distinction between the two. Enough confusion has existed between them, however, to indicate that constant care must be exercised in order that one generation after another not find itself committed to mere externalities rather than to the heart of divine revelation. Israel lacked an experiential committal to a living faith—not because she desired such a drastic void but because she had confused the outer form with the inner content.

It is no easier to distinguish the essential from the nonessential today than it was in the day of Amos. Yet, it is even more important for the Christian faith to make the proper distinction, since it holds that supreme revelation of God in Jesus Christ which Amos' generation did not have. It is of greater consequence today than in Amos' day that faith not be centered in external relationships.

Failure of Superficial Religious Form to Meet the Needs of the Heart, 5:21-27

As though to underscore the significance of making a proper distinction between the essential and the nonessential, Amos concluded by pointing out the failure of superficial religious form to meet the needs of the heart.

Rejection of ritual and worship as a means of justification and escape, 5:21-23, 25-27.—

> I hate, I despise your feasts.
>   and I take no delight in your solemn assemblies.
> Even though you offer me your burnt offerings and cereal offerings,
>   I will not accept them,
> and the peace offerings of your fatted beasts
>   I will not look upon.
> Take away from me the noise of your songs;
>   to the melody of your harps I will not listen (5:21-23).

At this point Amos shared the spirit of other eighth-century prophets who also condemned the ritual and worship they saw. Isaiah could speak of insincere worship as a "trampling of my courts" and commanded the people on behalf of God:

> Bring no more vain offerings;
>   incense is an abomination to me.
> New moon and sabbath and the calling of assemblies—
>   I cannot endure iniquity and solemn assembly.
> Your new moons and your appointed feasts
>   my soul hates;
> they have become a burden to me,
>   I am weary of bearing them (1:13-14).

Jeremiah in a latter day condemned the superficiality of worship in his day (cf. Jer. 7:1 ff.; 6:20 ff.). Malachi in a still later time did also (cf. Mal. 1:8 ff.), although the attitude of Malachi and other post-exilic as well as exilic prophets was much more friendly towards the cult than that of the pre-exilic prophets. There is no question but that the prophets condemned superficial ritual and worship as it was carried out in their respective eras.

The relevant question at this point, however, is: "Did Amos condemn ritual and worship, as such?" Did he mean to imply that formulated worship in terms of prescribed ritual should be abolished? Nothing could be farther from the truth of Amos' emphasis. While many insist that he did condemn all ritual, the truth of the matter is:

It was not sacrifice and ritual themselves that Amos was denouncing, but rather the abuse of them. Amos did not explicitly deny that ritual has any place in religion although religion may do without it. But to substitute ceremonial for righteousness was to degrade the very idea of religion itself.[13]

Amos insisted that religion could exist without ritual (5:25-27), for sacrifices had not been offered in the forty years in the wilderness. He also pointed out that Israel would go into another bondage, at which time they would take up their idolatries—"Sakkuth your king, and Kaiwan your star-god, your images, which you made for yourselves"—and go away into exile. Israel had evidently corrupted worship not only by an emphasis upon the superficialities, but by attempting to blend the worship of false deities with the worship of Yahweh.

Such corrupted worship could never validly be interpreted to mean, however, that Israel had known God through its ritual. Indeed,

Amos certainly stresses the irrelevance of sacrifice to the main concern of religion. For him it is peripheral at best and insidiously dangerous at worst, for ritual has the habit of putting people into moral slumber so that thinking themselves fastidiously religious they did not hear the voice of Yahweh in its far-reaching demands.[14]

The prophets, Amos included, were not concerned with the abolition of cultic forms. They were concerned, and greatly so, with the purification of such forms. The prophets were not innovators of new forms of worship. They were reformers who called Israel back to the heart of cultic life, to the new heart and the new spirit, to the accompaniment of cultic acts with dedicated and wholesome lives.

Here, then, is to be found the amelioration of the tensions between the prophets and the current worship forms. They were not concerned with abolition of worship but with the purification of individual hearts and lives which, as today, would have automatically purified sacrifice and worship in Israel.

Release of justice and of righteousness must supplant religious formalism, 5:24.—In the very midst of his attack upon the super-

---

[13] Calkins, *op. cit.*, p. 28.
[14] Gottwald, *A Light to the Nations*, p. 286.

ficiality of worship, Amos confronted Israel with the solution of the dilemma which she faced. It was not the abolition of cultic forms that he demanded. His solution was not negative but positive. It was not what they should not do, but what they should be willing to do. Amos called for the release of justice and righteousness in the lives of Israelites to the extent that it would come forth as the waters of an everflowing stream—"Let justice roll down like waters, and righteousness like an everflowing stream" (5:24).

Literally, Amos called for justice and righteousness to flow forth as a "perennial" stream. The phrase "wet weather spring," used in many parts of the United States, characterizes what Amos did not want. Justice and righteousness are not to become characteristics of one's life only at times when all is prosperous and advantageous. It is easier to manifest these characteristics at one time than at another, but for the true Israelite there must be no variation in their manifestation. Only when religion is thus combined with morality does it represent true religion "before God and the Father." This is not to reduce the dimensions of Israel's religious faith to those of a "do-good society," or make of it a mere instrument of social progress. It is, however, to lift religion from the clutching grasp of a dead ceremonialism and ritual, divorced from life, into a vibrant way of life which confronts every disturbing crisis of human experience with the faith of a personal encounter with God.

The only escape for Israel, of any generation, is a reunion of morality and religion. Apart from this there is absolutely no hope. A superficial formalism dedicated to the traditions of the past will no more meet the crises of the twentieth century victoriously than they met the crises of Amos' day. The fatal result of forsaking God remains the same for every generation—destruction both from within and from without. If a generation could abandon the false concepts that lead to the forsaking of God, perhaps the sin of Israel could be avoided and contemporary religion could be wedded to morality. Unless this can find realization, however, there is no hope for any generation.

So long as religion and morality are divorced one must cry with Amos, "The land is dead. I know not when it died, but it is dead." Therefore, "I take up over you a lamentation . . . Fallen, no more to rise, is the virgin; forsaken on her land, with none to raise her up" (5:1-2).

7

At Ease in Zion

Amos 6:1-14

Life among Israel's corrupt and oppressive strata of society was characterized with four words, "at ease in Zion." Nothing could have portrayed the indolent and oppressive life of the day any more graphically than this. While the multitudes lay beneath the heavy yoke of a corrupt social system in which the farmer was cheated at the markets and the helpless were abused in the courts, the leadership of the nation was in a complete state of ease.

In a time of unprecedented prosperity the nation had reacted in such a manner as to merit unavoidable judgment at the hand of God. To this double emphasis of prosperity and judgment the prophet Amos gave himself with vehemence.

Unprecedented Prosperity, 6:1-6

The Israel of Amos' day knew a prosperity that had not been experienced since the days of Omri, perhaps not since the time of Solomon himself. Had Judah then been united with the Northern Kingdom, the territory of Jeroboam II would have rivaled the empire of Solomon. The enlarged geographical territory that did exist, however, was accompanied by prosperity of an unprecedented nature. Not since the division of the kingdom had the nation known greater material wealth than that which was hers during the eighth century.

Before it arrives, prosperity has a way of promising deliverance from every problem that irritates and chafes man. Once present, however, it is generally found that the same problems must not only be faced anew but are often present with renewed intensification. Increasing the abundance of man's possessions is not neces-

109

sarily the secret for the multiplication of his happiness. Indeed, prosperity has a rather strange way of being so abused as to bring about oppressive injustice on the majority, while the minority in-dulges itself at the expense of the less fortunate. The inherent failure of prosperity is not only in its utter inability to satisfy the deep needs of life, but in the simple fact that everyone cannot know its material blessings.

At least, this was the case in Israel. While the minority of the people knew a more abundant physical life than ever before, the in-crease of trade and other enterprises meant greater oppression on the part of many. The wealth of the large landholder was accom-panied by the poverty of the rural peasant. With the increase of the merchant and the tradesman, there was the emergence of an oppressed working class. With the wealth produced by foreign trad-ing, there was the unjust absorption of land holdings from the established families. Prosperity alone never solves the problems of society. It often not only intensifies the old problems, but raises new ones as well.

False sense of security, 6:1.—The first consequences of such an unprecedented prosperity was the false sense of security engendered by the abundance of Israel's possessions. Of this false sense of se-curity Amos could say,

> Woe to those who are at ease in Zion,
>   and to those who feel secure on the mountain of Samaria,
> the notable men of the first of the nations,
>   to whom the house of Israel come (6:1)!

To be at ease in Zion was not inherently wrong. Indeed, four of the five times that the word *shā'an* is used in the Old Testament it is used in a good sense. For example, it was said in Jeremiah 30:10 that "Jacob shall return and have quiet and *ease,* and none shall make him afraid" (cf. Jer. 46:27; Prov. 1:33). The only time that it appeared in an evil sense, the word was used by Jeremiah con-cerning Moab: "Moab has been at *ease* from his youth and has settled on his lees" (Jer. 48:11). It was not wrong "to be at ease." Quite to the contrary, this was the promise of God to the faithful remnant.

At the same time it is obvious that the phrase was used in a derogatory sense in Amos 6:1. When is it wrong to be "at ease in Zion"? It is wrong to be at ease in Zion, basking in unprecedented prosperity, when one's fellow Israelite is in the most extreme condition of want and need. It is a crime to be at ease in Zion at the expense of the less fortunate. It is reprehensible in the sight of God for a people to drink wine from bowls, eat the best from the flock and the herd (cf. 6:4-6), and at the same time ignore the cry of the oppressed, the downtrodden, and the outcast at one's very door. Whether to be at ease in Zion is wrong or not must always be determined by the conditions under which one is in this state.

Not only were the people "at ease," they had also begun to place their trust in externals rather than in God. This is always the subtle temptation attendant upon prosperity. The Hebrew text, translated literally, reads: "and the ones trusting in the mountain of Samaria" (6:1). Two things should be noticed. First, such an attitude in the face of plenty was continuous. Amos used a participle, indicating continuous action, to characterize the attitude of those described. Second, Amos spoke of "those who feel secure" (RSV), or "the ones trusting" in the mountain of Samaria. The word translated "trusting" is the Hebrew word *bātach*, a word used at least forty-two times to indicate the faith commitment of man to God (cf. 2 Kings 18:5; Psalm 9:10; Isa. 26:3-4). This was the type of confidence the people had in the external powers of the day. They *trusted* in the mountain of Samaria, the seat of government. Therein was confidence placed, not in a living fellowship with God. This is always the condemnation of prosperity and materialism. It all too often breeds a false sense of security.

To Samaria, the mountain in which the people had placed their confidence, the house of Israel came. It was at Samaria the capital that "the notable men of the first of the nations" were to be found. The people flocked to "capitol hill" to gather before the chief men of the day. Confidence had been placed in the political structures of the day rather than in the One who had led Israel forth from Egypt in the beginning. It is impossible to read this without feeling that one has read an ancient parable on modern life.

Yet, one should read of this flagrant display of misplaced confidence with the realization that within forty years this same mountain was destroyed by the army of Assyria. Such is the in-

evitable fate of yielding to a false sense of security engendered by
the accumulation of possessions. As Jeremiah was later to say of
such materialism, "in the midst of his days they will leave him, and
at his end he will be a fool" (Jer. 17:11). No more appropriate
evaluation has ever been made of the folly of adopting a false sense
of security because of physical prosperity—"at his end he will be
a fool."

Dismissal of serious thought, 6:2-3.—Prosperity caused Israel to
dismiss any consideration of the very chaotic and threatening times
in which she lived. The nation had become so preoccupied with
its own wealth and luxury that it did not give consideration to the
imminent fall of the nation. As Amos said:

> Pass over to Calneh, and see;
>   and thence go to Hamath the great;
>   then go down to Gath of the Philistines.
> Are they better than these kingdoms?
>   Or is their territory greater than your territory,
> O you who put far away the evil day,
>   and bring near the seat of violence (6:2-3)?

This context, as generally understood, indicates that Israel was to
consider the destruction of Calneh, Hamath, and Gath; then this
was to serve as a corrective example for her. The problem in this
interpretation centers in the fact that Calneh did not fall until 738
B.C., Hamath in 720 B.C., and Gath possibly in 711 B.C. These dates
are too late for the time of Amos, and the reference to their destruction must either be a later insertion or must refer to previous catastrophes in the respective cities. One other alternative is possible,
although it involves a different interpretation than customary. According to this Amos was saying:

Leaders of the chief of the nations (v. 1), consider almost any great and
prosperous lands with which Israel and Judah can reasonably be compared (of course excluding Egypt and Assyria). From North to South
are any states better than your kingdoms, or greater in extent?[1]

The emphasis of verse 2 centers, then, in the fact that of all com-

---

[1] Cripps, *op. cit.*, p. 203.

parable nations Israel had been blessed far beyond them all. Because of this, Israel's failure before God was the greater.

Such an interpretation is not only coherent, but (1) it resolves the problem of the three cities having fallen after Amos' ministry, and (2) the answer to the question of verse 2 can be given in the negative, which the text requires, without producing a contradiction—"No, you are not better than these cities; no, their border is not greater than your border."

Amos' point of contention with Israel manifested itself most pointedly in the fact that they "put far away the evil day, and cause the seat of violence to come near" (6:3, KJV). Insensitive to such catastrophe, Israel was so beguiled by her prosperity that she "put away the evil day." The Hebrew could also be translated, "You *drive away* the day of calamity." The word *ra'*, translated evil, may mean moral evil, but it more often means distress, adversity, or injury.

While, on the one hand, the nation "drove away the day of calamity," she "caused to draw near (the) seat of violence." The nation's leadership could put far away its own day of calamity, at the same time drawing near a seat of violence. The phrase "seat of violence" had reference either to judicial decisions or to acts of violence emanating, ultimately, from the throne. How strange it was that although the leaders of the day were always driving away from the consideration of the day of their own calamity, their very action actually hastened the day of that calamity.

Stranger still, modern man still becomes so deluded by prosperity that he dismisses any serious thought about his future. Man never wants to consider the "day of calamity." Always, the day of reckoning is postponed by a thoughtless generation. Those who rise to inject a note of warning are often either silenced or ignored. Yet, the day of calamity moves steadily onward. Prosperity has a way of deluding man and extracting from him any attempt to consider his inevitable fate. One cannot put off the day of calamity by refusing to consider its reality. One cannot simply hope that it will "go away." While man may refuse to give any serious attention to it, its reality is not thereby denied.

Gross and excessive indulgences, 6:4-6a.—Having been lead into a false sense of security by the prosperity of the times, Israel not only dismissed all serious thought but gave herself to unprecedented luxuries and abandoned herself to flagrant indulgences. At no point in Old Testament literature is there to be found so vivid a description of luxurious and perverted social life as in Amos 6:4-6. This denunciation was simply a continuation of the attack upon the leadership of Israel. The word "woe" that appears in the Revised Standard Version of Amos 6:4 does not appear in the Hebrew text. The Hebrew begins verse 4 with a participle as it continues the description already begun in chapter 6.

In a vivid and pointed manner Amos cataloged the current indulgences of the day, condemning the excessive luxuries of the era. Taken in isolation from the context and viewed with moderation, no single act described was illegal. Neither the existence of beds and couches, the eating of animals from the flock and the herd, the singing of songs and playing of instruments, the drinking of wine, nor the anointing with oil was prohibited by Old Testament lawgiver, psalmist, or prophet. If this was the case, what then was the burden of Amos' attack? The prophet was concerned with the gross and excessive indulgences of the people. In the midst of their prosperity the notable people of the day (those described in 6:1 remain the subect in 6:4 ff.) had given themselves to luxuries unheard of in the rather simple background of their ancestors.

Archaeologists have unearthed vivid reminders of Amos' ancient denunciation of those who "lie upon beds of ivory, and stretch themselves upon their couches" (6:4a). The following evaluation of the "Samaria Ivories" illustrates the passage quite well:

The recent expedition found hundreds of fragments scattered over almost the entire city, but especially in the north-central section of the rectangular acropolis. They were, as a rule, smashed into tiny atoms, but many were fairly large. Evidently they had been used as inlay on furniture and on wooden walls. Amos (6:4) denounces the luxury of Samaria's couches of ivory. A Hebrew historian (1 Kings 22:39) refers to the house of ivory which Ahab built, perhaps a pavilion or reception hall having walls inlaid with ivory. Amos (3:15) scornfully predicts its destruction. . . . Description can give no adequate idea of the delicacy and beauty of these pieces.[2]

[2] Chester C. McCown, *The Ladder of Progress in Palestine* (New York: Harper & Bros., 1943), pp. 197-98.

The word "stretch themselves" is from *sārach*, which means "poured out."[3] The phrase could, therefore, be literally translated "and ones poured out upon their couches." The picture is that of one so overcome that he is simply draped across the couch.[4] The idea to be conveyed is that of one completely without control.

Conditions were so prosperous and luxurious that the upper classes ate "lambs out of the flock, and the calves out of the midst of the stall" (6:4, KJV). Meat was not ordinarily a part of the Israelite menu. Only the occasion of a notable guest called for the slaughter of an animal so necessary for producing milk products or wool (cf. Gen. 18:1-7). By the time of Amos, however, luxury was so rampant that not only was meat included in the diet of notable families, but only the very best was served. Meat was taken from the select of the flock. It also came from the calf that had not been allowed to run free but had been kept in a pen to insure greater delicacy. Such food was far removed from that of the average peasant or laboring man in Amos' day.

With a sarcastic thrust, Amos also ridiculed the music that accompanied such revelries, referring to those "who sing idle songs to the sound of the harp" (6:5). The verb translated "who sing idle songs" is a participle that occurs only here in the Old Testament. Its precise meaning is uncertain but the Septuagint translated the phrase as "those who rattle [*epikroteō*] to the sound of the musical instrument." Driver, after an extended discussion of the Hebrew verb *pārat*, concludes:

It is just possible that . . . it might be used of those who *extemporized* poetry over-rapidly, without premeditation, in a hurried flow of unmeaning, unconsidered words: Hence R.V. *sing idle songs*.[5]

This much is certain: the word is not the one normally used in the sense of "making music." They did not really make music, according to Amos, they simply beat upon or picked at the stringed

[3] S. P. Tregelles (trans.), Gesenius' *Hebrew and Chaldee Lexicon to the Old Testament Scriptures* (Grand Rapids: Wm. B. Eerdmans Publishing Co., 1957), p. 595.

[4] The word is also used with the meaning to overhand, go free, go unrestrained. Cf. Brown, Driver, and Briggs, *op. cit.*, p. 710.

[5] *Op. cit.*, p. 241.

instrument. In addition to this, everyone wanted to be "a little David," since David was recognized as the most significant of Israel's musicians (cf. 1 Sam. 16:18). Amos condemned his people by saying "like David invent for themselves instruments of music" (6:5).

Disdaining the ordinary cup or goblet, the people of the day drank from bowls. The Hebrew word translated "bowls" is *mizrāq*, and is used in a religious setting in every instance except Amos 6:6. At times the word has reference to the large bowls used in the ritual of sacrifice (cf. Ex. 27:3; Num. 4:14; 1 Kings 7:40). At other times the word is used of the large bowls containing flour and oil given by the princes (Num. 7:13 *et al.*), or the gold basins for temple use (2 Kings 12:13; Num. 7:20). Amos thus made a double thrust at Israel as he emphasized both the quantity of wine consumed and the desecration of the bowls which were intended for holy usage (cf. 2:8 which is set in the context of a shrine or temple).

Those denounced by the prophet were also guilty in his sight of having anointed themselves with "the finest oils" (6:6). In every instance except here the word anoint (*māshach*) is used in a religious or semireligious sense. In 6:5, however, the context indicates that the deed involved was the luxurious manner in which the costliest of oils were used for the people.

At a time when many were downtrodden and oppressed in the social upheaval of eighth-century Israel, there were still those who could use prosperity for gross and excessive self-indulgence. The simple background of an Amos had little place for indulgent dignitaries sprawled upon their elaborate couches, eating the best from the herd. John Edgar McFadyen suggests:

We see great social and political dignitaries indolently lolling on their gorgeous ivory-inlaid couches, feasting like gluttons, drinking wine greedily, not from slender cups, but out of capacious bowls, perfumed like dandies, revelling in improvised music of voice and instrument, but caring nothing for the people who were broken by the vices of peace.[6]

The words of Amos at this point are so relevant that, if it were not for certain distinguishing points, one might feel that he had read a description of contemporary society. Modern America may

---

[6] *The Use of the Old Testament in the Light of Modern Knowledge* (London: James Clarke & Co., n.d.), p. 211.

have foam rubber sofas instead of ivory inlaid couches, filet mignon steak rather than the lamb from the flock and the calf from the stall; but it has succumbed to the same temptation as did Israel. Wine may not be consumed in temple bowls any longer, but the per capita consumption of alcohol in America today would startle even an Amos. The "jukebox" may have displaced the *nevel* of Amos' day, but raucous music has remained to identify a society gone mad with self-indulgence. Luxury-minded society still anoints itself with the finest of cosmetics, despite the passage of twenty-seven hundred years. In essence, nothing has really changed in this world except the date on the calendar!

Complete unconcern for and indifference to the needs of others, 6:6.—From the Old Testament point of view what was wrong, with the exception of overindulgence, in the existence of ivory couches, meat on the menu, the making of music, the drinking of wine, or anointing with oil? The answer is, "Nothing!" At least there was nothing wrong on the surface. The contention of Amos was that such self-indulgence was wrong not only because of its excessive nature, but primarily because of the unconcern shown for others by those who so indulged themselves. In all of her prosperity and self-indulgence Israel was not "grieved over the affliction of Joseph" (6:6b).

The expression, "ruin of Joseph," is to be understood as a reference either to the military and political ruin of the Northern Kingdom or to the social oppression of the day. In this sense it repeats the emphasis made earlier upon the fact that all serious thought had been dismissed by the leaders of the nation. Prosperity and self-indulgence had made Israel insensitive to the deep needs of the people, who after all bore the brunt of every national calamity. No more devastating accusation could have been made, then or today, than that the leaders had become so engrossed in their own luxurious self-indulgence that they no longer cared for the people. One writer observes,

All these pieces of luxury, corrupting and effeminate as they are, might be permitted, but heartless indifference to the miseries groaning at the door of the banqueting-hall goes with them. "The classes" are indifferent to the condition of "the masses."[7]

---

[7] Maclaren, *op. cit.*, p. 168.

No man has the right to live in luxury while his fellowman lives in poverty.

Unavoidable Punishment, 6:7-14

Inordinate luxury in the face of such social needs as those to be found in Israel, could not escape the judgment of God. If there is a God who acts in the light of moral principles, then such a society cannot endure indefinitely. Amos knew and was himself committed to such a God as this—the God of the biblical revelation.

Exile is inevitable, 6:7.—Having once known the reality of God's true nature, every man should agree with Amos that Israel "shall go away captive." The Hebrew vividly portrays the departure into exile, "Therefore now you will go away captive at (the) head (the) captivity." As the long procession made its way into exile, the leadership of Israel would stand at the head of the column. No longer would they know their orgiastic feasts. For, translated literally, "the revelry of those sprawled out has turned aside."

Little did those who first heard these words realize how soon this would come to pass. With the fall of Israel in the last quarter of the eighth century, the words of Amos were literally fulfilled. Twentieth-century society would do well to take note of this, for

the connection between morality and prosperity on the one hand, and, on the other, between sin and decay can be traced more easily in the lives of nations than in the lives of individuals. History can be adduced to support the thesis that righteousness exalts a nation and unrighteousness destroys it. The evil consequences of collective sin are obvious. A nation with the rich given to luxury, the poor condemned to misery, and the rulers heedless of their responsibility, or even practicing oppression, will collapse through inner corruption or fall an easy prey to attack from without.[8]

Extent of the punishment, 6:8-11.—The extent of Israel's punishment is to be seen most vividly in that (1) it was grounded in God's person (6:8), (2) it governed the action of the people (6:9-10), and (3) it came in such a way that the great were equated with the small (6:11).

To know the wrath of a man or a nation can be a terrifying ex-

---

[8] Israel I. Mattuck, *The Thought of the Prophets* (London: George Allen & Unwin, 1953), pp. 125 f.

perience to either an individual or to a group. Such wrath is
generally tempered by the awareness that it is temporal and will
pass, or else that even in such dire circumstances one can still know
God. But Israel could know neither of these since her punishment
was grounded in the person and character of God. Because of this,
her punishment was not altogether temporal. In its midst she did
not know the comforting presence of God. "The Lord God has
sworn by himself," proclaimed the prophet (6:8). God had taken
an oath or, literally, "sworn himself," and in view of this obligation
he would act upon Israel's sin. Not by some external power had
he sworn, but by his own nature and character. This judgment arose
out of the character of God as an expression of his being.

Since judgment was the outgrowth of God's being, it was only
natural for Amos to say for God, "I abhor the pride of Jacob, and
hate his strongholds; and I will deliver up the city and all that is
in it" (6:8). Nothing is more abominable before God than pride.
Whether it be intellectual, moral, or religious pride, God abhors it
above all else. The word "pride" is translated in Jeremiah as the
"*swelling* of the Jordan" (KJV).[9] Pride that swells man like a flooded
river valley is despicable before God.

Along with pride, God "hated" the palaces of Israel. Built at the
expense of an oppressed and underprivileged people, Israel's elaborate buildings stood as living testimonials to a corrupt social order.
One wonders if the twentieth-century home, at times costing a total
of six figures, is any more acceptable than were the inordinately
elaborate buildings of Amos' day. Both pride and a corrupt social
structure brought about Israel's downfall. For, said Amos, "I will
deliver up the city and all that is in it."

Judgment based upon the nature and person of God is more
dreadful than anyone could imagine. The source of judgment
should affect greatly one's response to it. Amos contended that judgment was ultimately an expression of God's person.

Once judgment had fallen, said Amos, man's action would be
governed by it in all his life. He expressed this in the following
words:

---

[9] *Gā'ōn* is often used in the sense of the majesty of the Jordan, i.e., the green
and shady banks, etc. But Ewald takes the word in Jeremiah 12:5 to mean
"the *swelling* of its agitated waters." Cf. Brown, Driver, and Briggs, *op. cit.*,
p. 145.

And if ten men remain in one house, they shall die. And when a man's kinsman, he who burns him, shall take him up to bring the bones out of the house, and shall say to him who is in the innermost parts of the house, "Is there still any one with you?" he shall say, "No"; and he shall say, "Hush! We must not mention the name of the Lord" (6:9-10).

After having known tl e terror of war, men would experience its accompaniment—plague. Conditions would then be such that when a man's nearest relative came with another man who would burn the dead, they would not even speak the name of God for fear of bringing even greater calamity. The statement on burning has reference either to the practice of burning funerary spices or to cremation. Since cremation was not practiced in the Old Testament under normal conditions, it is to be assumed that a plague had smitten the city, thus necessitating the cremation of the bodies. While the burning of spices is not impossible, it does seem improbable.

The central emphasis of the prophet was the fact that judgment had been so real as to govern even idle conversation. After having known the reality of destruction, every action would be controlled by God's judgment. Driver indicates:

The relative of a deceased man enters his house to perform the last duties to his corpse. He finds no living person in it except one, secreted in a far corner, who tells him he is the solitary survivor of the household. So desperate is the outlook that men dread even to mention God's name, lest it should call down a fresh judgment on them.[10]

In such a time of judgment as that depicted by Amos, no difference would be made among the people. "For behold," said Amos, "the Lord commands, and the great house shall be smitten into fragments, and the little house into bits" (6:11). The prophet equated the great and the small before God. In his estimation both extremes, the great and the small houses, would be smitten. Destruction by warfare constituted God's judgment.

Explanation of punishment, 6:12-14.—Such punishment as that described by the prophet was further explained from two points of view. First, the cause of such punishment was summarized (6:12-

---

[10] *Op. cit.,* p. 200.

13). Second, the effect of such destructive judgment was portrayed (6:14).

Judgment was brought about, first, by *contradictory* action: "Do horses run upon rocks? Does one plow the sea with oxen? But you have turned justice into poison and the fruit of righteousness into wormwood" (6:12). The word translated "rocks" is not plural in the Hebrew but singular. It is a word (*sela'*) which means a cliff or crag in a literal sense (Ex. 17:6; 1 Sam. 14:4), or it may be figuratively used of Yahweh. It is used in the literal sense only of a cliff or rocky crag. Amos raised this question, "Are men so foolish as either to run a horse upon a rocky crag or over a cliff?" The answer is an obvious "No." No one would be so foolish. He then raised another question, "Do men plow the sea with oxen?" The answer is negative, for nothing could have been more foolish.

While men have had more common sense than to do either of these, Amos concluded that they did not have enough insight to act responsibly in other areas. "But you have turned justice into poison and the fruit of righteousness into wormwood" (6:12). Nothing could have been any more contradictory than this contrasting action. Any Israelite would have had enough sense not to have run a horse off a cliff, or to have attempted to have plowed the sea with oxen. At the same time, Israel did not apply the same responsibility to the "weightier matters" of justice and righteousness. How strange it was that men could act so responsibly in the common events of life, yet exhibit such irresponsibility in the more significant areas of human conduct.

Second, punishment came upon Israel because of her conceited arrogance. Of the people Amos could say, "you who rejoice in Lo-debar, who say, 'Have we not by our own strength taken Karnaim for ourselves?'" (6:13). The phrases "Lo-debar" and "Karnaim" have reference either to actual conquests, to Israel's dependence upon idolatry and her own strength for her deliverances, or to a combination of both.

The phrase "Lo-debar" may be translated literally as "not a thing" or "a thing of nought." Such references are often made to idolatry and would have been clearly understood by Amos' audience. The word "Karnaim" meant "horns." As such it may be used as a symbol of deliverance, because of the practice of giving refuge to the man who held to the horns of the altar. In Amos 6:13 it has reference to deliverance "by our own strength," and it was because of this arrogant attitude that judgment fell.

There are those who feel that "Lo-debar" and "Karnaim" are place names and refer to conquests made by Israel. Such sites can be located and this interpretation does not violate the central message of the prophet. If the double reference is historical, then Amos may well have spoken with a touch of sarcasm to this effect: "So, you have taken Karnaim and Lo-debar!" But underneath there is a sarcastic wordplay which implies that Karnaim (their strength epitomized in the conquest) is a *thing of naught* (or "Lo-debar").

Devastating and inevitable punishment is always brought about by the senseless, contradictory action of men and their accompanying conceited arrogance. When men apply greater reason and insight into the common deeds of riding a horse and plowing oxen than they do to the matters of justice and righteousness, judgment is inevitable. When men rejoice in their idols and glory in providing their own deliverance, judgment will always fall in history.

Affliction at the hand of an invading army would constitute the nature of God's judgment. Its effect would be seen in tribulation throughout the farthest reaches of the nation.

> "For behold, I will raise up against you a nation,
>   O house of Israel," says the Lord, the God of hosts;
> "and they shall oppress you from the entrance of Hamath
>   to the Brook of the Arabah" (6:14).

The action of God is more vividly portrayed in the Hebrew text than in the Revised Standard Version, although the latter should not be said to be in error at this point. The text reads: "Behold me! causing to rise up upon you." The finite verb is not used, the personal pronoun and participle having been substituted for it.

Amos also used a causative stem, "*causing* to rise up," which underscored the causative action of God. The prophet graphically called: (1) Behold me! (2) *causing* (3) to rise up (4) a nation. The affliction portrayed by Amos would reach from the extreme north to the extreme south of Israel as she existed at the height of her geographical expansion. "They shall afflict you," said the prophet, "from the entrance of Hamath to the Brook of the Arabah."

Our society is still "at ease in Zion." Both politically and religiously, individually and corporately, the message of Amos is still quite relevant. Society knows today an unprecedented prosperity. It faces at the same time an unavoidable and unparalleled punishment unless twentieth-century prophets can call men from their ease to a new committal to God. Amos could not do this for Israel. Can prophets of today succeed when he failed? Time alone will tell.

8

Faith in Conflict
Amos 7:1-17

Faith in terms of life commitment is no more immune from conflict, strife, and pressure than is any other area of life. It must face realistically the same questions, the same pressures, and the same fears that other facets of life confront.

Through a series of visions (7:1-9) and a historical interlude (7:10-17), a picture of the struggle faith encounters was presented by the prophet Amos. This manifested itself in two separate areas. First, in 7:1-9, the picture of faith in conflict on a national level is portrayed. The reality of a locust plague (7:1-3), a drought (7:4-6), and the destruction of a building (7:7-9) produced in the mind of the prophet the conflict of faith with catastrophic forces on a national level. Second, in 7:10-17, faith in conflict is set forth in its personal dimensions. Amos and his own faith commitment came into direct conflict with the priest Amaziah, exponent of institutional religion. The three visions epitomize the pressure applied to faith by circumstances of a national character; the encounter with Amaziah portrays the personal aspect of conflict on the part of a faith commitment to God.

Trying the Patience of God, 7:1-9

Faith was revealed as "faith in conflict" during the effort of Amos to avert national calamity through plague (7:1-3), drought (7:4-6), and warfare (7:7-9). In a time of intercessory prayer Amos revealed the struggle of faith with destructive national forces. At the same time, the intercession of the prophet revealed with clarity the manner in which one can "try the patience of God" by repeated intercession, apostasy, and further appeal. Such vacillation as de-

124

picted in Amos 7:1-9 presses the patience of God to its utmost endurance. The visions take on a twofold thrust: (1) they portray the faith of man in conflict with destructive national forces, and (2) they depict the exhaustion of God's patience.

Forgiveness, 7:1-3.—Threatening the welfare of the entire nation, a catastrophic locust plague had settled upon the fields of Israel. Such devastation as they normally worked was intensified, said the prophet, since their appearance came at the time of the latter mowing—after the king's mowing. Such a calamity could only have been overcome through the greatest of hardship and suffering.

The conditions which characterized the plague of locusts intensified the needs of the day, and heightened the conflict between faith and experience. The locusts were in the larval stage (4:9 has a different word for locust) and "were being formed" (a continuous, active participle) by God himself. As Harper states:

> The appearance of the larvae of the locust in the beginning of the coming up of the aftergrowth, and of fully developed locusts after the king's mowings, is intended to represent a destruction of herbage which threatened to be complete, since the latter appeared at a time when the rains were all past and the summer heat was just beginning.[1]

One can imagine the increased destruction likely to have been produced by the full-grown locusts as they ravaged the land. Not only was this true, but they were discovered during "the latter growth after the king's mowings." The expression was literal,[2] and had reference to the king's levy upon the spring cutting for his cavalry (cf. 1 Kings 4:7; 18:5).

In view of this, the confession of Amos concerning Israel's deep need is the more easily to be understood. "How can Jacob stand (or rise up)? He is so small!" In phrasing such a question Amos recognized the complete inability of Israel to rise up again, should the full force of the locust plague be directed upon the land. The prophet used a word that can be translated "rise up," and the phrase may be translated with this emphasis—"How can Jacob rise up, or recover, after such a plague as this?"

The cry of the prophet, in view of these circumstances, was one

---

[1] *Op. cit.,* p. 161.
[2] Some feel that the experience was used symbolically for the Assyrians.

for forgiveness. "O Lord God," cried Amos, "forgive, I beseech thee!" The Hebrew word *sālach* is translated in English as "forgive." The root meaning of the verb *sālach* is that of forgiveness or pardon in the more technical sense; it has no other meaning. (Cf. 1 Kings 8:30,39; Exodus 34:9; Jeremiah 5:1,7; 31:34. The word is always used of God's action, never of man's action.

The consequence of the prophet's petition was to be seen in the response of God of whom it was said, "The Lord repented concerning this; 'It shall not be,' saith the Lord" (7:3). For some, to speak of God as having repented, immediately precipitates a host of problems concerning the character of God.

Such difficulty as may be occasioned by the reference to the "repentance" of God may be alleviated by at least two considerations. First, God is often described in anthropomorphic terms within the Old Testament. To speak of God in such human terminology as "repentance" should not, therefore, occasion any great surprise or disturbance. Indeed, man can utilize only human concepts and ideas to describe the divine nature and character of God. These are all that he possesses. Such concepts, limited by their human frailty, often fall far short of encompassing the totality of God's nature and character. But this is simply one aspect of the difficulty involved in a divine-human encounter.

God is often portrayed in the Old Testament as writing (Ex. 31:18), sitting and resting (Gen. 2:2; Psalm 47:8), clapping his hands (Ezek. 21:17), whistling (Isa. 7:18), and laughing (Psalm 2:4). Also, he is characterized by emotions and attitudes that are quite human: he rejoices (Deut. 28:63), grieves (Gen. 6:6), feels regret (Gen. 6:6), is angry (Ex. 15:7), is disgusted (Psalm 106:40), is zealous (Ezek. 20:5; 34:14), or hates sin (Deut 12:31).[3] In such cases the Scripture writer sought to emphasize only one aspect of the human emotion or action ascribed to God. He does not intend to ascribe to God every possible connotation of the word utilized. In Amos 7:3 the writer sought only to point out that God had changed his mind or his intention concerning Israel (cf. Jer. 18:7 ff.), not that God had repented in the same sense that man at times experiences a moral transformation.

---

[3] Paul Heinisch, *Theology of the Old Testament* (Collegeville, Minn.: The Liturgical Press, 1950), p. 66.

In the second place, a proper understanding of the word translated "repent" in Amos 7:3 should clarify the problem of ascribing "repentance" to God. The word *nācham* is used at least thirty times of God in the Old Testament, the Revised Standard Version variously translating it as "repent," "to be sorry," "relent," or "change his mind." The basic meaning is that of a change of mind or purpose:

And Samuel did not see Saul again until the day of his death, but Samuel grieved over Saul. And the Lord repented that he had made Saul king over Israel (1 Sam. 15:35).

So the Lord said, "I will blot out man whom I have created from the face of the ground, man and beast and creeping things and birds of the air, for I am sorry that I have made them" (Gen. 6:7).

> For this the earth shall mourn,
> and the heavens above be black;
> for I have spoken, I have purposed;
> I have not relented [*nacham*] nor
> will I turn back (Jer. 4:28).

The word seems to convey the idea of sorrow or regret over a particular turn of events, associated basically with the idea of consolation and comfort whether directed inwardly toward one's self or outwardly towards others. Indeed, the preponderant usage of *nācham* is not with regard to "repentance" but comfort. This is the case of Psalm 23:4: "thy rod and thy staff, they *comfort* me."

The word is seldom used of man, occurring only in about five instances in the sense ordinarily connoted by the word "repent." Job responded to Yahweh, for example, by saying, "Therefore I despise myself, and repent in dust and ashes" (42:6).

Jeremiah used the word twice in the following passages:

> I have given heed and listened,
> but they have not spoken aright;
> no man repents of his wickedness,
> saying "What have I done?" (Jer. 8:6).

> For after I [Ephraim] had turned away I repented;
> and after I was instructed, I smote upon my thigh;
> I was ashamed, and I was confounded,
> because I bore the disgrace of my youth (Jer. 31:19).

Two other verses in the Old Testament make reference to man's repentance in terms of *nācham*, although they do not state that man has repented. "And also the Glory of Israel will not lie or repent; for he is not a man, that he should repent" (1 Sam. 15:29).

> God is not man, that he should lie,
>   or a son of man, that he should repent.
> Has he said, and will he not do it?
>   Or has he spoken, and will he not fulfil it? (Num. 23:19).

Used of God's activity some thirty times and of man's activity fewer than five, the word *nācham* should be understood in terms of what it meant for God to repent, not in terms of what it meant for man to repent. The majority (references to God) should define the meaning for the minority (references to man). God sets the pattern for the understanding of repentance. We must not judge God according to repentance as it relates to man; rather we must evaluate man's repentance against the background of God's repentance.

In seeking to understand Old Testament references to the repentance of God, far too many tend to do so against the background of what it means to "repent" in terms of the moral transformation demanded of men in modern ecclesiastical structures. Interpreted against the background of what it meant for God to repent, the word "repent" (*nācham*) means essentially a change of attitude or mind. This may on occasion involve a turning (*shūv* in the Hebrew text, *apostrephō* in the Septuagint), but this is secondary to the basic concept of repentance as a sense of sorrow or regret which produces a change of mind. Thus, the biblical concept puts far greater emphasis upon the inner attitude.

Forgiveness was a living reality in the mind of the prophet. His experience should serve as a source of continuing encouragement to modern man whose own faith may be in conflict with the catastrophic powers at work in society. As Luthi has observed:

What an encouragement that is for all who share in the mystery of intercession! Where a peasant from the edge of the desert is on his knees, there decisions can be made about a whole country. Where two hands are folded together, this most secret of actions can come to have a significance for world history. For God's government of the world is not automatic. God hears His servants when they call to Him, and the weeping of His children touches His heart. He holds the reins of world events with a loose wrist. He permits Himself to be moved to desist from wrath. In His wrath He is alterable. He is without "variableness of shadow of turning" only in His eternal mercy. "The Lord repented for this: it shall not be, saith the Lord."[4]

Familiarity, 7:4-6.—Because of the agrarian structure of society, drought was one of the most feared calamities of the ancient Near East. Its dire consequences often prompted the Old Testament writers to associate it with the judgment of God (cf. Amos 4:7-8; Jer. 14:1-6). Amos attributed the drought to the direct action of God, saying:

> Thus the Lord God showed me: behold, the Lord God was calling for a judgment by fire, and it devoured the great deep and was eating up the land. Then I said,
> "O Lord God, cease, I beseech thee!
>   How can Jacob stand?
>   He is so small!"
> The Lord repented concerning this;
>   "This also shall not be," said the Lord God (7:4-6).

The prophet probably witnessed the devastation of a literal drought, although there are some who contend that it was an actual fire or that it had symbolic reference to the Assyrians. In view of Amos' treatment of a literal drought in 4:7 ff., it would seem that 7:4 ff. is simply a parallel account.

By the use of figures of speech Amos described the intensity of the drought. It was so fierce, he said, that it had eaten, or devoured, "the great deep and . . . the land." In Hebrew, the phrase, "the great deep," is *tᵉhōm* which is the same word as in Genesis 1:2. In both cases the reference is to the watery chaos common to ancient Near Eastern thought. It was this chaos which was conquered in creation, although it continued to exist deep beneath the earth following creation (cf. 7:11; 8:2; 49:25; Job 38:16; Psalm 104:5-6). The fiery drought had consumed even this primeval deep, said the prophet, and had then devoured the earth.

---

[4] *Op. cit.,* pp. 98 f.

In the face of this adversity Amos did not pray for God to pardon, as he had done formerly. Rather he cried out, "Cease, I beseech thee!" The Hebrew word *chādhal* used at this point means actually "to cease" or "come to an end." At no point was the word ever used with the idea of forgiveness. An examination of the forty-nine occurrences in the Old Testament shows conclusively that it never has the connotation of pardon or forgiveness. It never means any more than "cease" or "come to an end." *Chādhal* is used with a variety of different connotations in the Old Testament, however, but primarily with the idea of "leave us alone." For example, Exodus 14:12 states: "Is not this what we said to you in Egypt, '*Let us alone* and let us serve the Egyptians?'" The consciousness of sin which prompted the cry for forgiveness (7:2) did not bring forth a comparable plea in the latter reference (7:5). Rather, the cry is simply that God would stop or "leave us alone!"

Familiarity inevitably has substituted *chādhal*, "leave us alone," for *sālach*, "forgiveness." Whether the prophet himself reflected such familiarity with God in his choice of words may be questioned. It could well be argued that his cry is still a petition, despite the fact that its content was not centered in forgiveness. Yet, even a prophet is not immune to familiarity with God. Consequently, every man of God would do well to guard against making common that which is holy. Otherwise, one may well move beyond forgiveness into familiarity, from penitence into presumption.

That Israel had become presumptive in its relationship with God should be obvious from the testimony of the prophets (cf. Amos 4:4 f.; 5:4-7; Hos. 5:6-7). Every generation is susceptible to the same error to which Israel had succumbed. Forgiveness can so easily be corrupted into familiarity. Indeed, unless one is quite careful, the forgiveness of sin can be perverted into a license to sin.

Failure, 7:7-9.—A man held a plumb line along a wall one day, and as the prophet beheld this common event the Spirit of God somehow impressed him with the fact that God also was holding a plumb line alongside Israel. It was in this that the revelation of God first gripped the heart of Amos. The plumb line was simply a string with a weight fastened to one end. When the string was held up to a wall, the weight caused it to hang in an absolutely vertical position. One could tell by this method whether or not a wall was leaning, whether it was safe or dangerous. The plumb line was taken from its literal usage and applied by the Old Testament writers as a figure of judgment (cf. Isa. 28:17; 34:11; Lam. 2:8; 2 Kings 21:13).

And the Lord said to me, "Amos, what do you see?" and I said, "A plumb line." Then the Lord said,
   "Behold, I am setting a plumb line
      in the midst of my people Israel;
      I will never again pass by them;
   the high places of Isaac shall be made desolate,
      and the sanctuaries of Israel shall be laid waste,
      and I will rise against the house of Jeroboam with the
         sword" (7:8-9).

God stood as a builder, said Amos, to test the character of the nation Israel. He would not be arbitrary in his decision concerning its fate. He would first set an absolute standard alongside Israel's deeds. Then he would determine his action by her conformity or lack of conformity to that divine standard. Every generation should behold the plumb line set in its midst, the absolute standard given of God by which humanity is held accountable. That Israel failed to meet the test of God's measurement was obvious in the prophet's immediate denunciation of both the religious structures ("high places" and "sanctuaries") and the political machinery ("the house of Jeroboam"). The wall built by the people in Israel was "out of plumb" and ready to topple over. Because of this, "I will not again pardon them any more." Literally, Amos said, "I will not go on passing over him." The phrase is much like that of Paul who could say, "The times of ignorance God overlooked, but now he commands all men everywhere to repent" (Acts 17:30).

In Amos' third vision God emphasized, without allowing the prophet to speak, that he would not again forgive Israel. God is a God of patience, and he does not come in judgment without a purpose. Yet, neither of these emphases abrogates the fact that there is a point beyond which God, because of his own character, either does not or cannot go in dealing with man's sin.

To every man and to every nation there comes a time when the plumb line has been set. Judgment moves on with its inevitable tread and nothing is left for man's degenerate condition but judgment in the historical progression of time.

Man's faith does find itself in conflict with catastrophic forces of national dimensions. Not only for Israel of Amos' day, but for modern man as well, the turbulent events of history try faith to the very limits of its endurance. Such trials may lead to forgiveness. If this be the result, then the conflict will have been purposeful and strengthening. Faith in conflict may also lead, however, beyond forgiveness to familiarity and eventual failure. This is the tightrope on which man must walk. Only a fine line separates the two areas of forgiveness and familiarity. The mark of a mature faith is to be seen in its ability to walk this tightrope—with no net below. One must walk the fine, keen edge that separates forgiveness from familiarity. This is no easy task. Yet, it is a necessary one and to this the mature man must commit himself.

Religion: Institutional and Experiential, 7:10-17

The interpersonal aspects of faith in conflict were depicted in the encounter between Amos and Amaziah. In this historical interlude in the midst of the five visions, the faith of Amos is seen to be in direct struggle with the power of institutional religion. Out of this conflict between the prophet Amos and the priest Amaziah, certain incisive and pungent insights are gained into both institutional and experiential religion.

Exponent of institutional religion: Amaziah, the priest, 7:10-13.— Both the priest and certain prophets had long been associated with governmental power in Israel (cf. 1 Kings 22:1 ff.; Jer. 26:7 ff.). As a result of this close identification between the government and religious leadership, a type of institutionalized religion far removed from the ancient faith of Israel had been produced. It was against this form of religion that successive generations of prophets found themselves in perpetual conflict (cf. Amos 4:4 f.; 5:4 f.; Hos. 4:4-9; Mic. 3:5-6; Isa. 1:12-15; Jer. 7:1 ff.; 23:1 ff.; 26: 7 f.; Ezek. 34:1 ff.).

During the course of his preaching Amos was overheard by Amaziah, priest at Bethel. Immediately upon hearing the denunciatory messages of the prophet, Amaziah reported Amos to king Jeroboam, saying,

Amos has conspired against you in the midst of the house of Israel; the land is not able to bear all his words. For thus Amos has said,

> "Jeroboam shall die by the sword,
>   and Israel must go into exile
>   away from his land" (7:10-11).

Not content with reporting Amos to the king, Amaziah proceeded to order Amos out of Bethel. The action of Amaziah reflected two aspects of institutional religion in every generation. First, it revealed its association with governmental power, as represented in Jeroboam II. Second, the attitude of institutional religion toward prophetic religion is also set forth with clarity.

In its association with governmental power, institutional religion manifested at least three definite characteristics. These attributes cannot be limited to the time of Amos; they appear whenever religion becomes institutionalized. The reason for this continual appearance seems to be the fact that the greater the degree of crystallization and organization on the part of religion, the easier it is to manipulate and to control such a rigidly structured religious form. The more rigid and concrete the religion, the easier it may be perverted for degenerate purposes.

First, institutional religion is responsible to a power other than that of Yahweh. In the case at hand, religion was responsible ultimately to the king. The first recorded action of Amaziah, the priest, was to report to Jeroboam (7:10a). Institutional religion is never free. It is inevitably subverted to governmental power, social structures, or to its own leadership. The danger in current denominational structures lies in the possibility of producing a religion which is responsible ultimately to its own headship. When religion is institutionalized there is always a "Jeroboam" rather than God to whom it is responsible.

Second, institutional religion favors the status quo and brands as conspiratory any prophetic message which brings corrective criticism. Viewed from the divine perspective, the words of Amos could hardly be classed as antagonistic to the will of God. Yet, Amaziah could say, "Amos has conspired."

The priestly function was largely fulfilled by protecting the past. For example, the priest was responsible for the preservation of the law that had been given. In the ritual he re-created in the present the past events of God. In all of this he fulfilled a wholesome purpose, for the present can be understood only in the light of the past.

The priests erred, however, in assuming that God had already completely revealed his will. Man, therefore, had only to ask what had been done. Such reliance upon the status quo developed to the point that the people could say of Jeremiah, "Come, let us make plots against Jeremiah, for the law shall not perish from the priest, nor counsel from the wise, nor the word from the prophet. Come, let us smite him with the tongue, and let us not heed any of his words" (18:18). This attitude reached its apex following the exile. By the time of Jeremiah, religion consisted almost entirely of an institutionalism which maintained the status quo at any expense.

Any generation which feels that it has a complete understanding of God would do well to read afresh the prophets of the Old Testament. To be sure there is for the Christian a note of finality in the ministry and person of Jesus Christ. Yet, even here one would do well to walk with care lest he should come to feel that the faith has been appropriated totally without error on his own part. Such an attitude represents an almost irresponsible pride. No man can be content with the status quo and what Isaiah called a religion "learned by rote" (Isa. 29:13). Indeed, every generation must hear, in terms its own age can comprehend, the unsearchable depths of God's revelation in Christ. Weston cites Wendell Phillips in saying:

No matter whose the lips that would speak, they must be free and ungagged. Let us believe that the whole of truth can never do harm to the whole of virtue; and remember that in order to get the whole of truth you must allow every man, right or wrong, freely to utter his conscience, and protect him in so doing.[5]

Institutionalized religion is not willing to allow such freedom of thought forms. It was not willing to do so in Amos' day. It will not do so today. This is its condemnation!

Third, institutional religion is required by its very nature to refrain from all criticism—saying, "Peace, peace, when there is no peace" (Jer. 6:13-14, etc.). Because of this, such religion rejected any contradictory word from God concerning the nation (7:10). The entire context indicates that Amos' message as reported by Amaziah (7:11) was not the type of message the priest would have

---

[5] Sidney A. Weston, *The Prophets and the Problems of Life* (Philadelphia: The Judson Press, 1932), p. 37.

given. Indeed, the words of judgment by Amos upon Jeroboam were declared by Amaziah to have been part of a conspiracy against the king (7:10). Institutional religion could not afford to allow criticism such as that offered by Amos, since the fate of such a religious structure was tied directly to the governmental evils denounced by the prophet. Such religion, in the very process of becoming institutionalized, sets up its own external marks of success which are considered infallible. Anyone, even an Amos, who dares to prophesy that such marks of externality do not necessarily reflect divine approval, runs the risk of expulsion to Judah (7:12).

"O visionary," said Amaziah, "go, flee away to the land of Judah, and eat bread there, and prophesy there; but never again prophesy at Bethel, for it is the king's sanctuary, and it is a house of royalty" (7:12-13). Interestingly enough, Amaziah did not address Amos with the customary title for a prophet—nāvî'. Instead he referred to him by the older term, chōzeh, which may well be translated, "visionary." There is little place in institutional religion for the visionary—the crude fellow who can never stay within the accepted bounds of "navi-ism" as the professional prophets of the day. Amaziah commanded the "visionary" Amos to leave the temple at Bethel immediately. After all, it was the king's sanctuary, or holy place—a house of royalty, or a royal house. In this attack upon Amos, the priest Amaziah reflected three continuing attitudes of institutional religion toward prophetic religion.

First, institutional religion assumes that prophetic religion is irrelevant to both the locale and the situation. In effect it was saying, "Go someplace else to prophesy." Bethel was located in the Northern Kingdom. Consequently, Amaziah said to Amos, "If you must prophesy, go back to the south, eat your bread there and [literally] play the prophet there." Throughout the history of Israel institutional religion contended that prophetic religion was totally irrelevant. Prophetic religion was always "out of place" in the mind of institutional religion.

One can trace the same pattern in the attitude of the established church throughout the history of the Christian faith. Whether it be the established church in terms of its Roman development, by virtue of national associations, or in terms of denominations that have grown powerful in influence, rigid institutionalism has continued to deny that prophetic religion is relevant either to the particular area or to the problems faced. This attitude is confronted on a contemporary basis when one hears such statements as: "preachers ought to preach the gospel and leave other issues alone," or "the church doesn't have any business in politics" (or racial tensions, or anything else except the maintenance of the status quo). Inevitably, there is always the Amaziah who, while he may not deny the right to prophesy, indicates that it should be done in other locales, in other social situations, or in other religious structures. The more rigid the institutionalism, the greater the insistence that prophetic religion is irrelevant both to geographical locale and to the situation at hand.

Second, institutional religion assumes that prophetic religion must be isolated since it has no rights of accepted status (7:13). The point made by Amaziah was not that Amos did not have the right to prophesy. Indeed, it is generally granted that any prophet of Israel had the right to appear at a sanctuary and gain a hearing. Amaziah did contend that prophetic religion as represented by Amos had no accepted status at Bethel. What Amos did in Judah was one thing. What he did at Bethel, the king's sanctuary, involved entirely different considerations.

This has been the history of prophetic religion from the Old Testament, through the New Testament, and into the modern era. Institutional religion has always tended to carry with it a protective shell which insists upon its own superiority, on the one hand, while it denies the right of prophetic religion to speak, on the other. Those who are part of the free church today, and who identify themselves with prophetic religion as epitomized in Amos, are indebted beyond measure to the host of men who have not been willing to accept the premise that prophetic religion must not speak because it does not have the status of institutional religion. Just as the early disciples—unlettered in many cases and often socially belittled—the exponents of prophetic religion have continued to speak under the leadership of the Holy Spirit. "Uneducated, common men," they could do no less than "speak of what we have seen and heard" (Acts 4:13,20). Despite the refusal of accepted status, prophetic religion has denied its enslaved position and has spoken forth with clarity. It has recognized that

They are slaves who fear to speak
For the fallen and the weak;
They are slaves who will not choose
Hatred, scoffing and abuse,
Rather than in silence shrink
From the truth they needs must think;
They are slaves who dare not be
In the right with two or three.
                                        JAMES RUSSELL LOWELL

Third, institutional religion assumes that prophetic religion cannot be identified with true religion, can make no claim to validity, since it is not a "temple of the kingdom" (7:14). Institutional religion committed its most serious error, and thereby sowed the seeds of its own destruction, in its assumption that true religion can be identified only with the external forms prevailing at a given period of time. The assumption which Amaziah made was that Bethel (literally, "beth-el" which means "house of God") and its attendant liturgy was the only accepted way of revelation for Israel.

Any religious structure which adopts such a rigid, unalterable attitude toward the revelation of God has laid the foundation for its ultimate defeat. One of the primary laws of nature is that of adaptability. The organism which cannot adapt to its changing environment eventually becomes extinct.

This same principle must be applied to religious forms. This does not mean that religion must change the divine content of its heritage. It does mean that every generation must appropriate the revelation of God for itself in terms that its contemporaries can comprehend. For example, Amos did not seek to inaugurate a new covenant. But he very definitely tried to reform the faith of Israel in terms of both the old covenant and the contemporary problems of his own generation. H. Wheeler Robinson has stated concerning the present scientific age, "Scientific knowledge can never invalidate religious faith, however much it may lead to the restatement of the ways and means of God."[6]

Highly organized religion is not willing to make the concession that religion can be stated in more than one way. In fact, it cannot

---

[6] *Inspiration and Revelation in the Old Testament* (Oxford: At the Clarendon Press, 1960), p. 184.

make such a concession. It cannot for the simple reason that it has a religion "learned by rote" rather than through experience and can, therefore, do nothing except hold rigidly to the "temple of the kingdom." It does not know how to meet God afresh every day.

When the characteristics which marked the religion of Amaziah are manifested in contemporary religious structures, the death knell has been sounded. The thrust of ancient power may still orbit rigid institutionalism on its trajectory, but it no longer possesses the power for further thrusts. In the midst of a troubled and disillusioning world one wonders if institutionalism has not already slain many of the contemporary Christian movements supposedly characterized by a prophetic spirit. If this be the case, then the only hope lies in an honest reappraisal of such movements and a renewed dedication to the principles of experiential religion as manifested in the prophet Amos.

Epitome of experiential religion: Amos the prophet, 7:14-17.— "God has a few of us whom he whispers in the ear," says Robert Browning in "Abt Vogler." Herein is to be found the distinguishing mark between institutional and prophetic religion, for prophetic religion insists that "God whispered in its ear."

Thus, the conflict between institutional and prophetic experience, says Hastings, is

the contrast between a religion of externals and a religion of the heart, between ceremony and morality, between tradition and progress, between bondage and liberty, between the God who in ancient times has expressed Himself once for all, and the living God of To-day and To-morrow.[7]

If twentieth-century Christianity is to recapture the power of its first-century thrust, it must do so by honest rededication to experiential religion. In his encounter with Amaziah, Amos manifested at least three characteristics of a religion of experience.

First is the charismatic nature of the prophetic office (7:14). The term "charismatic" has been used to characterize those men and women who have been endowed with a particular "charisma," or gift from God. A detailed examination of the entire problem of the

---

[7] Edward Hastings (ed.), *The Minor Prophets* ("The Speaker's Bible" [Aberdeen, Scotland: The Speaker's Bible Office, 1930]), p. 85.

charismatic leader in Israel would be out of place in this study.[8] At the same time, attention should be called to the fact that throughout the history of Israel there was a twofold emphasis upon the nature of leadership. In many instances men, and at times women, rose up to serve Israel because of some special endowment on the part of God (cf. the judges). This endowment included, primarily, the possession of the Spirit. However, when the reference to Spirit fell into disrepute because of the ecstatic prophets, the possession of the word came to be of primary importance (cf. the use of the phrase "the word of the Lord" by the eighth-century prophets and their successors rather than an appeal to the Spirit of God).

Because of special gifts given by God, the judges ruled at different times in Israel. For some this endowment involved military ability, judicial insight, governmental sagacity, or even physical strength. What these men were, what they contributed, was built upon the fact that they possessed special gifts of God. One of the most critical periods in the development of such leaders came at the time when Israel repudiated charismatic leadership in favor of kingship (cf. 1 Sam. 8:4 ff.). This is not to say that none of the kings were charismatic, for many of them did have unique gifts bestowed by God (cf. Saul, David, Solomon). It is to say, however, that from the time of Saul forward, leadership in Israel was transmitted primarily through hereditary rights rather than by the endowment of a special gift from God.

Not only were kings selected according to hereditary rights, but the priests were also obtained in this manner. Many of the priests were no doubt godly men and meant much to Israel. At the same time they held an office and performed a service because of heredity rather than through the possession of charismatic endowments. The prophets in the tradition of Elijah, Amos, Isaiah, and Jeremiah, on the other hand, prophesied not because of any inherited status, but because of the conviction that God had called them. The recorded experiences of these prophets support this thesis.

Amos denied that he was a prophet because of associations with the cultic prophets identified with institutional religion. His was not the role of a court prophet or one who had a mission because

---

[8] Cf. Max Weber, *Ancient Judaism,* trans. and ed. Hans H. Gerth and Don Martindale (Glencoe, Ill.: The Free Press, 1952), pp. 11, 17 ff., 40, 98 f., 157, 294, 395 for a development of charisma in Israel.

of heredity. Rather, said he: "Not a prophet [am] I, and not a son of a prophet [am] I but a herdsman I [am] and a dresser of sycamores" (7:14). Disavowing any association with the professional prophets of the day, Amos stressed his former lay status in words that could not have been misunderstood. As Williams has observed:

He was the first layman to appear upon the scene of history with a religious message. This is not to denounce all professional religious leaders . . . but here is testimony that great religious insight is not confined to the professional leaders of religion . . . the minister of religion is not a priest who has been trained to techniques, practices, and dogmas of an institutionalized religion. He is a man who has found satisfaction in the religious way of life and is seeking so to share his experience with others that they may make the same discovery for themselves.[9]

In a day when the ministry tends toward a cold professionalism, the message of Amos carries a severe warning for the contemporary minister. Prophetic religion must always be charismatic, forever remaining dependent upon the gifts of God for its vitality. Otherwise it would cease to be prophetic religion. Prophetic religion finds both its motivation and its consuming power in God-given endowment, not through ecclesiastical position or inherited status.

Second is the compulsive power of a divine conviction (7:15). The initiative behind Amos' prophetic ministry lay in the conviction that God had called him forth to the office of prophet. After having stressed his status as a shepherd and as a dresser of sycamores, Amos insisted that "the Lord took me from following the flock, and the Lord said to me, 'Go, prophesy to my people Israel.' " Thus, the prophet correctly discerned the hand of God as the initiating factor in his prophetic ministry. As Karl Barth says of Paul's call to apostleship, so one might say of Amos at this point:

Here is no "genius rejoicing in his own creative ability" (Zundel). The man who is now speaking is an emissary, bound to perform his duty; the minister of his King; a servant, not a master. However great and important a man . . . may have been, the essential theme of his mission is not within him but above him—unapproachably distant and unutterably strange.[10]

---

[9] *Op. cit.*, pp. 158-59.
[10] *The Epistle to the Romans*, trans. Edwyn C. Hoskyns (London: Oxford University Press, 1953), p. 27.

Today, every major Christian communion faces the problem of a decreasing number of young men entering the ministry. It should never be forgotten, however, that the initiating factor in prophetic religion must be in the call of God, not in the promotion of men. One of the most tragic turn of events current denominations could ever face would be that of perverting the call of God into no more than a psychological response to high-pressure salesmanship in order to create ministers for empty pulpits.

In recognizing the divine element as the initiating force in his ministry, Amos also declared the purpose of God to have been the proclamation of his word to the people. The word translated "prophesy" in Hebrew is "to be prophet." The verb is a denominative; its meaning is determined by the nominative, or noun. In this case the noun determines the meaning of the verb. The Hebrew word normally translated "prophesy" actually means "be a prophet." In fulfilling this role the prophet spoke the revelation which had come to him. Yet, a close study of the prophet will reveal that in "being a prophet" he did far more than speak words. At times he symbolically acted out the message (cf. Isaiah, Jeremiah, and Ezekiel). At other times he served as political counselor, as in the case of Isaiah, but at all times he manifested a way of life that distinguished him from the false prophets of the day. To be a prophet involved more than merely speaking words. Many contemporary prophets have yet to learn this, but it was inherent in the ministry of the Old Testament prophets.

Prophetic religion discerns the hand of God as the initiating factor in the prophetic ministry. At the same time, however, it declares the purpose of God to be the proclamation of God's word or revelation, through the one who is to "be a prophet unto my people." To a greater or lesser degree this same mission can be filled in the life of every man who is committed without reservation to the same God who called Amos. George Adam Smith has observed:

To see the truth and tell it, to be accurate and brave about the moral facts of our day—to this extent the Vision and the Voice are possible for every one of us. Never for us may the doors of heaven open, as they did for him who stood on the threshold of the earthly temple, and he saw the Lord enthroned, while the Seraphim of the Presence sang the glory. Never for us may the skies fill with that tempest of life which Ezekiel beheld from Shinar, and above it the sapphire throne, and on the throne the likeness of a man, the likeness of the glory of the Lord. Yet let us remember that to see facts as they are and to tell the truth about them—this also is prophecy.[11]

Third is the committal of the prophet to his task despite the hostility of institutional religion (7:16-17). In the face of such imposing opposition, a man of lesser stature would likely have capitulated at the first onslaught of Amaziah. The withering attack of the priest, coupled with the threat of governmental retaliation, would no doubt have forced the resignation of men lacking the compulsive power of a divine conviction. Yet, Amos knew that God had called him to his task, and to this call he remained faithful. Rather than retreat by fleeing into the Southern Kingdom as the priest had suggested, Amos continued his attack.

The faithfulness of the prophet to his divine purpose reflected itself in the fact that Amos proclaimed God's word despite the power of institutional religion which was exercised against him. As he continued his proclamation, he said:

> Now therefore hear the word of the Lord.
> You say, "Do not phophesy against Israel,
>   and do not preach against the house of Isaac."
> Therefore thus says the Lord (7:16-17a).

The very reminder that Amaziah had commanded him not to prophesy again in the name of the Lord was seemingly the catalyst that brought forth a final word of judgment, this time upon the priest and his family.

Amos incisively pointed out the fate of the people, saying, "Your wife shall be a harlot in the city, and your sons and your daughters shall fall by the sword." No more terrible fate could have been held out for Amaziah. His wife would be reduced to the state of a harlot and his children would be slain in a time of warfare. Amos knowingly spoke of the ravages of war in his own and succeeding days. Nothing could have been more reprehensible for the priest than that his wife should occupy such a position in society. No threat could have been more real than that of warfare, for such had hung over Israel as some ominous cloud all of her existence.

---

[11] *Op. cit.*, I, 84.

The prophet also graphically portrayed the fate of the land. "Your land shall be parceled out by line," said the prophet. Land was treasured in such a manner in Israel as almost to be beyond modern understanding. One of the most grievous sins of a previous era had been the misappropriation of Naboth's vineyard for Ahab through Jezebel (cf. 1 Kings 21:1 ff.). In Israel not even a king was free to take the land of one peasant farmer without suffering prophetic condemnation. Laws had been given to insure the proper inheritance of land (cf. Num. 36:1 ff.), and in every way possible the value of family property had been underscored. It is against this background that one should read the threat to Amaziah that there would come the day when his land would fall beneath the surveyor's line and be given to other men than those of his own family.

In terms of the priest's death in another (unclean) land, Amos described the fate of Amaziah himself. Nothing could have been dreaded more than to have been removed from one's land and to die on foreign soil. The common belief of the day centered in the fact that God was limited to the land of Israel. While Amos did not necessarily accept this premise himself (cf. Amos 1:1 ff., 9:7), others no doubt did. David could speak of being forced to serve other gods should he be driven from the land (cf. 1 Sam. 26:19), and Jonah fled from the land because of a kindred idea. Naaman the Syrian vowed that from the time following his encounter with God through Elisha that he would serve no god but Yahweh. To enable him to do this in Syria he urged that he be given "two mules' burden of earth; for henceforth your servant will not offer burnt offering or sacrifice to any god but the Lord" (2 Kings 5:17). Hosea pointed out that during a time of exile,

> They shall not pour libations of wine to the Lord;
>   and they shall not please him with their sacrifices.
> Their bread shall be like mourners' bread;
>   all who eat of it shall be defiled. . . .
> What will you do on the day of appointed festival,
>   and on the day of the feast of the Lord?
> For behold, they are going to Assyria;
>   Egypt shall gather them,
>   Memphis shall bury them.
> Nettles shall possess their precious things of silver;
>   thorns shall be in their tents (9:4-6).

No greater threat could have been placed upon a priest than exile to a foreign land where he would not only die, but in the interim would not know the cultic practices which for so long had been a vital part of his life. This was to be judgment of Amaziah.

Finally, Amos briefly indicated the fate of the entire nation by saying, "and Israel shall surely go into exile away from its land" (7:17d). Words of judgment and condemnation spoken upon the nation by the prophet were to find their literal fulfilment within the lifetime of many who heard his words. The destruction of the Northern Kingdom as an empire in the last quarter of the eighth century B.C. should serve as a constant reminder for those who find it difficult to believe that history can serve as the arena for national retribution.

Thus it was that the prophet committed himself to his task despite the hostility of institutional religion. Society never ceases to need men of integrity who cannot be intimidated, coerced, or threatened into silence at the very time when a prophetic voice is needed most. Here is to be found the acid test of prophecy. Will a man speak for God in the face of adversity and hardship, even the threat of both job and life? Knudson has well observed:

Someone has said that there are two classes of preachers—the good preachers who have something to say, and the poor preachers who have to say something. But there is yet another and higher class. It consists of those who both have something to say and who have to say it. Such are the prophets. Such a one was Amos.[12]

---

[12] *Op. cit.,* pp. 65-66.

9

The End Has Come
Amos 8:1-14

One of the most frighteningly disturbing events upon which an individual can contemplate is "the end." Whether it be the end of human existence as known in this life, the end of the cosmos as often stressed in some eschatological forecasts, or the end of an era of vitality for an institution; "the end" is never a pleasant topic of conversation. Consideration of its reality is intensified in its sense of dread, however, when one comes to understand that "the end" is not just a future event. It is a present, existential relationship in which every man is involved. "The end" is not an event that will transpire "some day"; it is an experience in which every man participates in the here and now. The "end" is a present reality. You are there. In some strange and mystical way, the future merges with the present and every generation shares in "the end."

Amos anticipated this when he spoke of the end as having already come upon Israel. The end of the nation had been so firmly fixed that he viewed it as already achieved. The nature of her character and her reaction to God had been such that Amos could speak of the end of Israel as a present reality. Therefore he stated, quite pointedly, "The end has come upon my people Israel"(8:2). In elaborating upon the "end" for Israel, Amos dealt with three major emphases: (1) the revelation of the end for Israel (8:1-3), (2) the reason for the end of Israel (8:4-6), and (3) the reality of the end for Israel (8:7-14).

Revelation of the End for Israel, 8:1-3

In the fourth of a series of five visions, the prophet interpreted symbolically a basket of summer fruit which he had seen, perhaps

145

at a local market place. Utilizing this medium, he attempted to impress upon the people the fact that even as the end had come for the current crop of fruit, it also had already come for Israel. The vision was a revelation of the end for Israel.

Inspiration of the Prophet, 8:1-2a.—Although both the inspiration and the authority of the Bible are maintained as primary tenets of the Christian faith, seldom has any definitive statement been made concerning the method of inspiration. This vacuum exists because of the sheer impossibility of ever stating the precise details involved in the inspiration of a biblical author. In the visions of Amos, however, one is confronted with the place that common events of daily life played in the process of inspiration.

The origin of the prophet's inspiration lay with God. No matter how it may have been mediated, Amos could say with conviction, literally, "Thus the Lord Yahweh caused me to see." By using a causative stem of the verb, Amos underscored the fact that God was the causative factor in his inspiration. He did not say, simply, "I saw." Rather, he said, "He *caused* me to see!"

The organ of the prophet's inspiration was an event in everyday life—a basket of summer fruit. As he gazed upon the last of the crop, Amos was led to see that Israel was just like this summer fruit; her end had come. Other men had seen the fruit as had Amos, but they had not spoken the revelation of God. What made the difference? The difference lay in that somehow or other the Spirit of God laid hold of Amos, as it did not with others, so that he "saw" what others had failed to see: the analogy between the summer fruit and the life of the nation.

The organ or medium of revelation in the Old Testament was often an event quite common to the life of the prophet. Thus it was that Jeremiah saw the rod of an almond *(shāqēd)* and was reminded that God was watchful *(shōqēd)* over his word (Jer. 1:11-12), the boiling pot facing from the north (Jer. 1:13-15), and the activity of the potter which led him to perceive the sovereignty of God (Jer. 18:1 ff.). Amos also received needed stimulation through the observation of common sights in Israel (cf. Amos 7:7). Thus, in the fourth vision he saw a basket of summer fruit *(qāyits)* and was reminded that the end *(qēts)* had come for Israel. Both the sound of the related words and the sights of the fruit provided the stimulus for God's revelation.

The oracle of the prophet's inspiration assumed the form of these words addressed to his people, "The end has come upon my people Israel; I will never again pass by them" (8:2a). The oracle given by the prophet was divine in both origin and authority. Despite its human mediation, it called for a response from Israel with all the authority of God. Although the divine element in inspiration should never be deleted, neither should the human aspect be ignored. Just as both the divinity and the humanity of Jesus must be maintained in a proper view of the incarnation, the dual nature of the Bible must also be preserved. In the two thousand years of her history, the Christian faith has declared heretical any view of Christ which has denied either side of his dual nature. The same principal should certainly be applied to God's Word as well. The Bible is both human and divine.

Interpretation of the event, 8:2b-3.—The end had come for Israel, proclaimed Amos. Never again would God pass over her and ignore her sin. The verb used by Amos was a perfect, *bā'*, indicating completed action: the end had already come. The Hebrew concept of time did not involve the consideration of its linear progression so much as it did its inner content, or what took place within the time process. While the modern man may speak of "time marching on," the ancient Hebrew had no such concrete view of time. Time for him was known by its content, and primary consideration was not given to verbal tenses of past, present, or future. Hebrew verbs cannot indicate by their structure any element of time; they can only indicate whether an action was incomplete or complete in the mind of the writer (cf. pp. 29-30). Amos was so convinced of Israel's "end" that he could say "it has already come."

When current political and religious structures are examined, one often has this same feeling concerning the present reality of the end. It seems as though the end has already come. The multitudes do not know it, but the battle is over; the finish line has been crossed; the end is already present. The seeds of dissolution and destruction have been sown in both political and religious life, and the end is here—now! No one has expressed this more vividly for the church than has Karl Heim who says:

The Church is like a ship on whose deck festivities are still kept up and glorious music is heard, while deep below the water-line a leak has been sprung and masses of water are pouring in, so that the vessel is settling hourly lower though the pumps are manned day and night.[1]

The endurance of God's patience had been exceeded, claimed Amos. So much was this a fact that he could say, "I will not continue any longer to pass over him" (i.e., Israel, 8:2c). Because of this, the judgment of God would fall, and the songs of the temple or better palaces would be exchanged for wailings. These wailings described by Amos constituted a part of burial ceremonies in Israel, and had become a prophetic symbol of lamentation for the nation.

The extent of the disaster described by Amos was to be seen in that dead bodies would be multiplied throughout the land: "The dead bodies shall be many" (rav happeger, 8:3). No doubt Amos had in mind some catastrophic national calamity in time of war.

The extremity of this disaster was further to be manifested by an oppressive silence that would hang over the land (8:3). The Hebrew of the verse is, "in every place he will cast silence." The Revised Standard Version translates this: "they shall be cast out in silence." Yet the verb is not passive, as in the RSV translation. The Septuagint translator rendered the verb with a first person pronoun (epirripsō siōpēn), supporting a translation, "I will cast silence." If this is followed in preference to the Massoretic text, which is rather difficult at this point, the meaning would be obvious: Yahweh himself would be the cause of the oppressive silence over the land. This alternative would fit well with the silence maintained in Amos 6:9-10 because of the fear that any violation of the silence by the mention of God's name would bring further wrath. It seems preferable to translate the phrase "I will cast silence," or "I will bring silence." The prophet sought to emphasize that a dread and awful silence such as characterizes any great calamity would engulf the entire land.

Such was the interpretation of the basket of summer fruit by Amos. By a blending of divine inspiration and the common life of man, Israel received the revelation of God. The end would not be some day, said Amos. With all of its attendant calamities, the end was already there as judgmental retribution. These words ring with

---

[1] *Christian Faith and Natural Science* (New York: Harper & Bros., 1953), p. 24.

a note of disturbing relevancy for the modern church. The end has come. The seeds of destruction have been sown; only heartfelt repentance and renewal can now avail. But even with this, the end has already come for many of our commonly known religious forms and structures.

Reason for the End, 8:4-6

Pessimism such as that manifested in the foreboding statements on the end for the nation Israel did not characterize a prophet of God without reason. While many in life are pessimistic by nature, this does not represent the normal outlook on life. Man by nature gravitates toward an outlook upon life which is optimistic and hopeful (at times this sense of optimism is perverted by a naivete which fails to reckon with sin and error). There was a definite reason for the prophet to adopt such a pessimistic evaluation of his nation. The vivid description of the present reality of a catastrophic end for Israel was not the result of cynical pessimism. Rather, it represented a correct evaluation of the future based upon an analysis of the present. The reason for "the end" of Israel lay in the area of social injustice and religious superficiality. These two prevailing situations were sufficient cause for Amos to realize that the end had come.

Social injustice as a principle, 8:4.—The prophet addressed Israel as those "who trample upon the needy, and bring the poor of the land to an end" (8:4). Religion unconcerned with the welfare of the underprivileged and the downtrodden has never walked side by side with an Amos of Tekoa, a Micah of Moresheth-Gath, or a Jesus of Nazareth. Social concern can, of course, be perverted into an ethic without a religion. At the same time, due care should be exercised lest in the process of life a religion without an ethic should be produced.

Amos called into account those who continually (as indicated by the use of the participle) "trampled upon the needy" (8:4). The root word *shā'aph* is translated "trample" in the Revised Standard Version on the strength of emending *shā'aph* to *shūph* (cf. 2:7 where there is Septuagint support for this). The Hebrew word *sha'aph* is used frequently in the Old Testament, however, and its use is quite satisfactory and its meaning clear in this context. Therefore, the word will not be emended but retained in the sense of those who pant after the poor with the idea of swallowing them up.[2]

The verb *shā'aph* (1) means to breathe hard, to pant, (2) means to catch with open mouth, and (3) is translated in Job 7:2 as "a slave who *longs for* the shadow."[3] Gesenius gives the following explanation, "to pant after any one is . . . to thirst for his blood, a metaphor taken from wild beasts," and cites Amos 8:4 as an example of such usage.[4] Men panted after the poor of the land as some wild animal of the jungle panted after its victim. At the same time, the prophet condemned in like manner those who "bring the poor of the land to an end." In both these instances social injustice as a principle of life and conduct was cited as characteristic of a nation of whom it could be said "the end has come." Whether it be ancient Israel embroiled in the problems of the eighth century B.C. or contemporary America, the principle is the same. Social injustice as an accepted fact of life will bring about the destruction of any society, ancient or modern.

Superficial religious experience, 8:5a.—Externally, religious life in the day of Amos was prospering as it had not for a considerable period of time. The high places were thronged with worshipers, sacrifices filled the altars of the land, and the sound of the ritual drifted upward toward God who neither heard nor cared for such superficiality. The crux of the religious problem in the day of Amos lay in the fact that although religious life was outwardly prosperous, inwardly it was dead and ineffective. Such superficial worship as was practiced could be characterized by a later prophet as merely the "trampling of my courts" (Isa. 1:12).

The superficiality of religion manifested itself, first, in a false interpretation, or attitude, toward sacred days. The merchants of the day observed the new moon and the sabbath, both of which were

---

[2] Since the word *shā'aph* appears in both verses, the translation of Amos 8:4 as "pant after" and Amos 2:7 as "trample" may appear arbitrary. Indeed the RSV consistently translates the two as "trample." The Septuagint treats the two differently (2:7 as *kondulizō;* 8:4, *ektribō*), however, and the phrase "upon the dust of the earth the head of the poor" found in Amos 2:7 does not appear in Amos 8:4. The rather simple construction of Amos 8:4, *hashō'°phīm '°vyōn*, lends itself well to the common usage of *shā'aph* (to pant after).

[3] Tregelles, *op. cit.,* p. 799.

[4] *Ibid.* Some emend *shā'aph* to *shūph* (to trample). Cf. 2:5.

THE END HAS COME

holy days in Israel. At the same time that they observed these days by either refraining from business practices, or witnessing less than normal traffic, they whined and complained, asking:

> When will the new moon be over,
>   that we may sell grain?
> And the sabbath,
>   that we may offer wheat for sale? (8:5).

Doing little if any business on religious days, the merchants of the day could not wait for the day to pass so that "business as usual" could be entered into once again. A day kept in such a spirit as this is no holy day. Indeed, the sin of man is compounded in keeping such a day insincerely, for in this he adds hypocrisy to a general lack of religion. As one writer observed,

These men, who were only fit to be swept out of the land, were most punctual in their religious duties. They would not on any account do business either on a festival or on [the] Sabbath, but they were very impatient till—shall we say? Monday morning came—that they might get to their beloved work again.[5]

The accusation of Amos against the superficial observance of holy days in the eighth century B.C. is strongly suggestive for the contemporary Christian observance of religious days. When the spirit of the day is lost in a superficial legalism, the individual is no better than the merchants condemned by the prophet Amos. Yet, for how many people is the observance of Sunday merely an enforced restraint because of custom or superficial commitment? The solution lies, however, not in an abandonment of the day, but in a re-examination of current attitudes, and a rediscovery of the day's true significance for the individual. The answer to hypocritical observances does not lie in the giving up of the day, but in the abandonment of the superficial religious attitude which produces hypocrisy.

Second, the superficiality of religion manifested itself in the failure to connect social justice as the corollary of religion. In this particular statement on social injustices the prophet was speaking to men who were externally religious. They were quite scrupulous in the keeping of both the new moon and the sabbath. Yet they

---

[5] Maclaren, *op. cit.*, pp. 171-72.

could take the remainder of life and use it to cheat and oppress
those weaker citizens of Israel. In this regard, it is to the continuing
shame of the Christian faith that in far too many instances those
geographical areas which manifest the greatest intensity of religion
are at the same time characterized by the greatest of social injustices. Religion has become superficial, to say the least, when it can
accommodate itself to dishonest business practices such as those
described by the prophet Amos.

   Specific social injustices, 8:5b-6.—Having indicted the merchants
of Israel for both social injustice as a principle in life and the superficiality of their religious experiences, Amos then proceeded to catalog the specific social injustices of which they were guilty. It was
from the average market place of the day that Amos took the examples of social oppression which characterized the land. The action
of Amos would parallel that of a contemporary prophet who might
proceed to list the specific dishonest business dealings carried out
by thoroughgoing church members.

   Reducing the measure stood at the head of the catalog of injustices compiled by Amos (8:5b). Throughout the history of Israel
the matter of honest weights and measures was constantly brought
to the attention of the nation. The law stated specifically, "You
shall do no wrong in judgment, in measures of length or weight
or quantity. You shall have just balances, just weights, a just ephah,
and a just hin: I am the Lord your God, who brought you out of
the land of Egypt" (Lev. 19:35-36; cf. Deut. 25:13; Prov. 20:10).
Despite the obvious instruction of the law and the prophets, Amos
could say of the merchants, they "make the ephah small and the
shekel great, and deal deceitfully with false balances."

   The ephah was a unit of measure containing about eight gallons.
If a man sold grain with a dishonest ephah, perhaps equipped with
a false bottom, he could realize a greater number of measures from
a given amount of grain than if he used the honest ephah. The
shekel, on the other hand, was a unit of weight, and the man who
purchased goods from the merchant had to give more silver to bal-
ance the shekel than if the shekel had weighed the correct amount.
"The merchant whose weights were heavier," says Gwynn, "would
extract from the buyer more money than his due; but not content
with that he gives him short weight of corn by using a measure that

was too small."[6] The third practice listed, dealing "deceitfully with false balances," was a general statement on the dishonest manipulation of the scales and is too general to be specifically identified. These dishonest practices enumerated by Amos involved one of two actions. First, they may have involved the actual alteration of the Israelite standard of measure. The ephah may have been equipped with a false bottom or in some other way made to contain less than a standard ephah. The shekel may have been deliberately made to weigh more than the standard. Gwynn says of this that "a quarter shekel weighing 39 grains instead of the proper 33 has been found lately on the site of Samaria."[7] Such archaeological evidence, if correct, illustrates the very practice cited by Amos.

A second suggestion has been made concerning the dishonesty found by Amos on the part of the merchants. Williams has suggested that the practice mentioned by Amos was one in which the merchants took advantage of the difference between the Babylonian and the Phoenician weights and measures. He has indicated that, "these were the two established standards in the Near East at this time. The one system had weights heavier than the other system, and it was one of the tricks of the trade in that day to buy using one system and to sell using the other, and so make extra profit."[8]

The latter possibility was just enough "within the law" to make it attractive to many merchants and, while it cannot be demonstrated conclusively to have been the practice followed, it offers an exceedingly probable alternative. The sin of the merchants, according to this, lay not in the overt type of dishonesty such as might characterize one who would falsify either the ephah or the shekel. The sin condemned was much in principle like many business transactions today in which the ignorance of the individual concerning banking or other financial matters is capitalized on. There was nothing "illegal" involved, and the merchants of Amos' day may well have said as many would today, "A man has to watch out for himself. I can't help it if he doesn't know enough about business dealings to protect himself." Despite the passing of almost twenty-seven centuries, the practice of merchants in the day of Amos are

---

[6] *Op. cit.*, p. 43.
[7] *Ibid.*
[8] *Op. cit.*, p. 156.

strikingly akin to those of many "respectable" businessmen, and church leaders, today. Men who would not overtly steal by using a false measure will quite willingly utilize technical intricacies of business to achieve the same results.

The purpose involved in the dishonest business transactions mentioned by the prophet was cited in these terms: "that we may buy the poor for silver and the needy for a pair of sandals, and sell the refuse of the wheat" (8:6).

The phrase, "buy the poor for silver and the needy for a pair of shoes," appeared earlier in the book of Amos (2:6) and is to be understood in generally the same manner in chapter 8 as in chapter 2.[9]

Society has, indeed, degenerated when the righteous man can be oppressed at the court of law because of silver handed over as a bribe against him. Yet, it should be remembered that

the pair of shoes, or rather the trifling sum that would buy them, was not the price of the person of the accused, but of the integrity of his judges. They were so corrupt that, for the trifling sum that his persecutor could afford to pay for judgment against him, they pronounced the innocent guilty.[10]

This remains a valid principle, for such bribery reflects not the price of the person oppressed, but the price of the integrity of his judges. The fraudulent wage given to the few that remain oppressed in the American labor market is not so much a reflection upon the ability of the oppressed as it is an indictment of the oppressor. It is not so much a reflection of the worth of the individual as it is an index to the worth of the one who pays such a wage. As McFadyen says,

It is no accident that those who do not love the Sabbath cheat on Monday: they rob God and their own souls one day, and their neighbor the next. To be irreligious is to be anti-social; to be religious, in the sense demanded by Hebrew prophecy, is to be social.[11]

In almost the same breath, Amos denounced those who were

---

[9] See pp. 38-39 of this book.
[10] Mitchell, *op. cit.*, p. 87.
[11] *Op. cit.*, p. 114.

willing to sell "the refuse of the wheat" to the poor, those who obviously were in no position to do anything about such mistreatment. The Hebrew is "and what falls (or is *caused* to fall) of (the) grain." Not content with having dealt in all of the dishonest ways indicated, the merchants of the day took the refuse of the wheat, containing the chaff left at the bottom of the container, and sold this inferior grain to the poor. The disparity between religious integrity and ethical principles in one's business dealings was thus underscored quite vividly. No doubt Amos would condemn inferior merchandise just as fervently in the twentieth century as he ever did in the eighth century B.C. Wrong is wrong, regardless of the century in which it may transpire.

Reality of the End for Israel, 8:7-14

With dark and somber words Amos portrayed the reality of Israel's doom. Her "end" was a reality which confronted her as an inescapable fact of history. Shrouded in the remoteness of the future, the end was such that Amos could speak of it in terms of present experience. It was with the intention of calling Israel back to God that the prophet depicted the "day of doom" which lay ahead for the nation. The emphasis was made in such a manner that Israel could not escape its horror. As Amos stressed, inevitable judgment must fall upon every nation that perverts life as Israel had done.

Determination of Yahweh constituted the ground for the reality of the end, 8:7-8.—The reality of the "end" for Israel lay in the fact that such a time of retribution had been determined by the action of God. "The Lord has sworn by the pride of Jacob," said Amos. "Surely I will never forget any of their deeds" (8:7). The fate of Israel was not settled by the action of the Assyrian power, said the prophet. God himself had taken an oath to the effect that he would never forget any of their deeds.

The phrase, "the Lord God has sworn by his holiness," appeared earlier in the book of Amos (cf. 4:2) but the phrase, "sworn by the pride of Jacob," is an unusual object by which God takes an oath. Lehrman suggests that "the self-esteem in which the aristocrats gloried was so constant that, ironically, God takes an oath by it."[12]

---

[12] *Op. cit.*, p. 117.

Such pride had become so much a part of life that its arrogant presence was assumed as always present. The tragic condition of the nation was thus further underscored as God recognized the pride of Jacob as one of the unchanging factors in all of Israelite society. Pride lies at the heart of all sin.

As a consequence of the oath that God had taken, "never to forget any of their works," Amos asserted, "Shall not the land tremble for this, and every one mourn that dwells therein, and all of it rise like the Nile, and be tossed about and sink again, like the Nile of Egypt?" (8:7b-8). Nature was quite often depicted both as suffering and as rejoicing in the life of man. At times earth bore the judgment with man and at other times she shared in his redemption. The prophet is to be understood metaphorically in this as in many other contexts, and the literalist misses the entire point of the passages under consideration if he looks for a literal fulfilment.

There is a sense in which the prophet was quite literal, however. This involved the earthquake that came in the second year of Amos' call (cf. 1:1). It should be remembered that the ancient Hebrew conceived of the earth as in the shape of a saucer, supported upon great pillars over $t^e h\bar{o}m$, the great, primeval deep. With this understanding of the nature of the earth, one can understand with greater ease the sheer terror that an earthquake would strike in the heart of ancient man. The earthquake can be an event of terrifying proportions for those of us today who understand at least something of its physical cause and limited effect. But for the Hebrew, who knew nothing of its physical cause, it seemed, no doubt, that at each moment the saucer-shaped earth would split apart and disintegrate. Little wonder that Amos could speak of the earth as rising and falling as the Nile did in flood stage, for in the earthquake the earth seemed to be no more than a chip floating on the great deep.

This ancient view of the world and the earthquake made it easier for the Hebrew to see the hand of God at work than for the modern. He is no less at work today, however, and modern man would do well to recapture the conception of a God large enough to control all physical forces of the entire universe and utilize them to his glory. For Amos the earthquake was simply the trembling of the earth at the voice of God as he determined, on the basis of his oath, never to forget any of the deeds of Israel. Modern man has correctly moved beyond this cosmological understanding of the universe. It is to be hoped, however, that he has not moved beyond God who is as much creator, sustainer, and redeemer today as he ever was in the day of Amos.

Disaster depicted in double symbolism, 8:9-10.—The disaster which was to come upon Israel in the course of history was depicted by the prophet in two symbols as the reality of the end was further manifested.

Cosmic reactions were to accompany the disaster of Israel, indicated Amos, for " 'on that day,' says the Lord God, 'I will make the sun go down at noon, and darken the earth in broad daylight' " (8:9). The turning of darkness into light was itself a mark of the power of God (5:8), but the end that was to come upon Israel was to be marked by an even greater phenomenon: the sun to go down at noon and the earth would be darkened in broad daylight. The casual reader of the book of Amos may well read this verse and conclude immediately that Amos was predicting some sign that will accompany the so-called "end of the world." Nothing could be farther removed from the purpose of Amos. To begin with, in Old Testament prophetic thought "the end" is an "end" in history and not some cosmic disintegration as a later apocalyptist may have envisioned. In the second place, the event portrayed by Amos was based, in all probability, upon the eclipse of the sun which occurred in 763 B.C. Having witnessed such a startling eclipse, the prophet later adopted this as one of the attendant signs of God's action. This time of chaos, when the sun went down at noon, would occur once again in Israel. This time it would be at the time of "the end," preceding in all probability the transformation of the earth.

Ceremonial reverses would also characterize this time of distress which would come upon Israel (8:10). To appreciate fully the relevancy of this threat one must understand what the ritual of Israel meant to the sincere worshiper. After all, the essence of everything in terms of worship that he could experience was bound in the ritual of the day. Whatever may have been its weaknesses it was, for the time being, man's ladder of access to God. It would have been an even greater loss for the Israelite to have been deprived of all ritual than it would be for the modern Christian to be deprived of every expression of public worship normally associated with the church. Against this background, one should read the words of Amos:

> I will turn your feasts into mourning;
>   and all your songs into lamentation;
> I will bring sackcloth upon all loins,
>   and baldness on every head;
> I will make it like the mourning for an only son,
>   and the end of it like a bitter day (8:10).

The feasts of the day would be turned into times of mourning and the songs into lamentations. The feasts whereby God was worshiped would become occasions for mourning. The songs of praise so often sung by individuals in Israel would become songs of lamentation. What reason was to be found for this reversal in Israel? Amos was trying to depict the sorrows that would fill the land because of death produced by the ravages of war. The reference to sackcloth and baldness, two signs of sorrow at death, would support this interpretation. The final threat centered also in the fact that it would be a time of mourning like the mourning of an only son, the most loved because of his uniqueness. The end of the entire matter would be a bitter day.

Nothing could have expressed more vividly the sheer terror of the end that Amos saw for the nation. A time of death and sorrow awaited Israel as some inevitable fate toward which she moved. Yet, in all of this the prophet held out no hope of altering the "end." In the mind of the prophet it had been set and could not be changed.

Devoid of the Word of God, the Land Knew Spiritual Famine, 8:11-12.—The famine of which Amos spoke at this point was, strangely enough, not a famine of food. Hear the prophet as he speaks:

> "Behold, the days are coming," says the Lord God,
>   "when I will send a famine on the land;
> not a famine of bread, nor a thirst for water,
>   but of hearing the words of the Lord.
> They shall wander from sea to sea,
>   and from north to east;
> they shall run to and fro, to seek the word of the Lord,
>   but they shall not find it" (8:11-12).

The revelation of God's word was to be suspended and no longer be available (8:11). When the prophets spoke for God the people often rejected their words. Earlier, Amos had said for God, "I raised up some of your sons for prophets . . . but you . . . commanded the prophets, saying, 'You shall not prophesy'" (2:11-12). Micah, a later prophet of the same century, could say of the people of his day, "'Do not preach'—thus they preach—'one should not preach of such things'" (2:6). Of Jeremiah, two centuries later, the people said, "Come, let us smite him with the tongue, and let us not heed any of his words" (18:18). This same pattern could be traced throughout the Old Testament into the New Testament and beyond it to the present day. No one really wants to hear a true prophet of God.

To those of Amos' day and to the hard of heart in every generation, the revelation is the same. Inevitably, there will come the time when you will welcome a word from God—a time of famine, neither of bread nor of drink, but of the hearing of the words of the Lord. How the times would change, for from the day of rejecting the word of the prophet there would come the day, said Amos, when men would wander from sea to sea in search of the word. The country would be examined from the north to the east for a trace of God's revelation.[13] Men would run to and fro to seek the word of the Lord, "but they shall not find it." "Try to imagine all the influence of religion taken out of your life. In trouble, sickness, loneliness, failure, try to imagine yourself cut off from God. This is what Amos prophesies. . . . Sin, whether national or individual, isolates a man from God."[14]

Note the reaction of Israel to such a state of famine (8:12). The value of the revelation of God was immediately recognized—but only after it was too late. It takes neither keen intellect nor deep spiritual perception to discern the value of God's word and influence when those are no longer available. Even the most skeptical individual present in America would recognize the tremendous contri-

[13] The unique phrase "north to east" may stem from the refusal of some scribe to allow "south" to stand, believing that it would be impossible for Judah to be the source of the word. The phrase "sea to sea" indicates east to west, and one would have expected "north to south" as the parallel, not "north to east."

[14] Kent and Smith, op. cit., p. 25.

bution of the Christian faith, even to his own way of life, if everything that Christ had contributed was immediately taken from him.

Little wonder that Israel responded by running to and fro in anxious search for the words of the Lord. From north to east she traveled and from sea to sea they searched for the revelation but it was not to be found. Only the south was overlooked in her search, perhaps because of the hostility between the two kingdoms.

Nothing could be more dreadful than to forfeit through self-inflicted neglect the opportunity of knowing the revelation of God as it was formerly known. This was the threat held out over Israel. This is the continuing threat under which every generation must live. One must never in prideful self-assertion take for granted the privilege of knowing God. It may always be available, but again, it may not.

Desperate condition reflected in the failure of the choice of the land, 8:13-14.—"In that day," said the prophet, "the fair virgins and the young men shall faint for thirst" (8:13). Even the best of the young people, those physically best equipped for such strenuous times, would not be able to survive. At this point it is not likely that Amos is to be understood in an absolutely physical sense. He did not envision a time when physical conditions would bring about the fainting of the youth in Israel. What he did portray were the deep spiritual needs through which the land would pass. He spoke of these needs in the terms of thirst, thus paralleling the previous mention of both spiritual famine and thirst in 8:11-12.

Amos' call was for Israel to prepare for the difficult days that lay ahead. Such days would be so desperate as to cause even those to faint who were best equipped to survive. In this time of desperate crisis and need, Amos emphasized that false worship would be of no help. Those who had sworn by "Ashimah of Samaria" would fall and never rise again.

The Revised Standard Version translation "Ashimah of Samaria" is best understood against the background of 2 Kings 17:30 wherein the numerous gods introduced into Samaria by Assyrian colonists are described: "the men of Babylon made Succoth-benoth, the men of Cuth made Nergal, the men of Hamath made Ashimah." If this is the proper translation, then either Ashimah had already begun to be worshiped in Samaria during or prior to the time of Amos, or the passage is an editorial addition after the action of the men of Hamath, described in 2 Kings 17:30, had already taken place.

On the other hand, it is also possible that the phrase *be'ashmath shōmrōn* means "by the guilt (or sin as the King James Version translates it) of Samaria." The Hebrew word *'ashmāh*, "wrong-doing" or "guiltiness," is the word in the text, and the translation "guilt of Samaria" is quite proper. In support of this position is the fact that "Ashimah" is a completely different word, *'ashīmā'* not *'ashīmāh*, that appears only in 2 Kings 17:30 and is otherwise unknown in the Old Testament. In addition, the Septuagint translation of the phase as *hilasmou* (atonement or sin-offering) lends strength to the present translation as "guilt of Samaria" rather than "Ashimah of Samaria" as in the RSV.

Amos did not, then, intend to refer to Ashimah of 2 Kings 17:30 as the RSV implies. He intended to stress the "guilt of Samaria," using this as a sarcastic means of referring to the calf worship of Samaria in which Yahweh was, in all probability, viewed as enthroned upon or above the calves. Yahweh was probably even envisioned as enthroned above the ark and the cherubim in the Jerusalem Temple (cf. 1 Sam. 4:4).

Not only would those fall who had sworn by the "guilt of Samaria," but also those who said: "As thy god lives, O Dan," referring to the other golden calf. These, together with those who had made religious pilgrimages ("as the way of Beer-sheba lives") to Beer-sheba would "fall, and never rise again" (8:14).

By this method Amos emphasized, as Jeremiah did later, the failure of false religious structures to meet the real needs of man. Jeremiah ridiculed the people of his day by saying,

> But where are your gods
>   that you made for yourself?
> Let them arise, if they can save you,
>   in your time of trouble;
> for as many as your cities
>   are your gods, O Judah (Jer. 2:28).

There was no hope for Israel because they had placed their confidence in substitutes for God that paraded in the disguise of Yahweh.

Throughout the entirety of chapter 8 there is no appeal for a return, and there is no hope of restoration and forgiveness held out to the people. It would be unwise to be dogmatic at this point, but in all likelihood they could not find a fresh revelation of God because they had given themselves to "the guilt of Samaria" and had said, "As thy god lives, O Dan," and "As the way of Beer-sheba lives" (8:14). As one writer observes:

Why was the search vain? Has not God promised to be found of those that seek, however far they have gone away? The last verse tells why. They still were idolaters, swearing by the "sin of Samaria," which is the calf of Beth-el, and by the other at Dan, and going on idolatrous pilgrimages to Beer-sheba. . . . It was vain to seek for the word of the Lord with such doings and worship.[15]

How disturbing and how relevant are these words to contemporary institutionalized religion, despite its organizational or denominational structure, that abandons the charismatic nature of experiential religion. To such ecclesiasticism the prophet still proclaims that the end has come. Indeed, religion which is superficial and false to the very core cannot be permanent. A religious structure produced by the pressures of man alone is already dead, although it may seem to breathe. Its end has come, for it has been dead from its beginning. These fearfully disturbing words should cause a probing of heart and a searching of motivation such as leads to a new reformation. Whether this will be accomplished or not, however, depends upon the candor, the courage, and the conviction of those who can hear the words, "the end has come!"

---

[15] Maclaren, *op. cit.*, p. 175.

10

Man's End as God's New Beginning

Amos 9:1-15

The religion of Israel did not grant immunity from judgment, and physical descent from Abraham did not guarantee exemption from accountability. Love is neither blind, nor is it weak. Consequently, the wrath in God's love and the love in God's wrath should be equally recognized. Judgment is never the last word in God's conversation, however, and either Amos or a later scribe also stressed the restoration of Israel from the chaos worked by judgment (9:8b-15). The message as now contained in Amos 9:1-15 lays strong emphasis upon the redemptive nature of judgment in history. Judgment falls even upon the people of God (9:1-8a), but in its wake the redemptive work of God is also to be seen as a reality (9:8b-15). In a very real sense, the end was but a new beginning for the people of God. This was true not only for Amos. For every generation God remains the "God of the new beginning."

Man's End: When Judgment Falls, 9:1-8a

In this final vision of the fivefold series (cf. 7:1-3,4-6,7-9; 8:1-3; 9:1 f.), Amos depicted the judgment of his people by the analogy of a building which was being destroyed. Quite likely Amos actually saw such a building, and as he witnessed its destruction God's Spirit led him to see that just as the building was being destroyed, Israel was also faced with imminent destruction.

Judgment is inevitable, 9:1a.—While men may "put far away the evil day" (6:3) for a brief period of time, judgment is inevitable and cannot be permanently frustrated. As a woman once said to a

AMOS AND HIS MESSAGE

French cardinal, "My Lord cardinal, God does not pay at the end of every week; nevertheless, he pays."[1]

Judgment originates in the action of God. "I saw the Lord," said Amos, "standing beside the altar, and he said: 'Smite the capitals until the thresholds shake, and shatter them on the heads of all the people'" (9:1a). Judgment is never the expression of human evaluation and action alone. It arises out of the character of a holy God and finds expression through his control of time and history. God is the God of history, and history is the history of God.[2] As such, history reflects God's action and ultimate control; it is not dominated solely by economic, social, or political forces. When judgment falls, let God be seen. Otherwise, it will have failed in its purpose.

Judgment originates at the house of God. Such sacrilege as that emphasized throughout the book of Amos made judgment inevitable. Men cannot go up to Bethel and Gilgal to sin rather than to worship and not know divine retribution. Whether in ancient or modern times, the church must stand responsible for her conduct and for her own intrinsic character. Even the temple and the church are not beyond judgment. Actually, the fact that they were, and are, the media of the divine revelation increases the degree of their responsibility. In the words of the New Testament, "the time has come for judgment to begin with the household of God" (1 Peter 4:17).

Amos knew that judgment had to fall upon the religious structure of the day. It was inevitable, for he had seen the Lord "standing beside the altar" proclaiming judgment. He had witnessed the smiting of the very capitals of the columns themselves and had beheld in a vision the roof crashing upon the heads of insincere worshipers. Nothing could have been clearer than the fact that the very inevitability of judgment stemmed, to a great extent, from the hypocrisy and superficiality of worship.

Judgment originates because of the people of God. "Smite the capitals until the thresholds shake," proclaimed the Lord, "and

---

[1] C. E. Macartney, *Chariots of Fire, and Other Sermons on Bible Characters* (New York: Abingdon-Cokesbury Press, 1951), p. 76.

[2] L. Gulkowitsch, *History as the History of Ideas with Special Reference to Old Testament and Jewish History* (London: Shapiro, Vallentine & Co., n.d.), p. 7.

shatter them on the heads of all the people." The "capitals" referred to were the tops of the columns supporting the roof. To smite them would have brought the entire roof crashing down "on the heads of all the people." The people themselves had brought about the inevitability of judgment. Sin is suicidal in nature and every ungodly act carried out in Israel bore fruit a hundredfold in terms of personal and national judgment.

Judgment is inescapable, 9:1b-4.—The assertion of the inescapable nature of judgment was clearly set forth in the words of the Lord to the effect that "not one of them shall escape" (9:1*d*). One of the tragic characteristics of man enmeshed in his sin is the feeling that somehow or other judgment can be escaped. Men today continue to say, as in the eighth century B.C., "disgrace will not overtake us" (Mic. 2:6). To these as to those of his own day, Amos would deny such assertions and proclaim with a later prophet of the same century,

> For the Lord of hosts has a day
>   against all that is proud and lofty,
>   against all that is lifted up and high;
>
> . . . .
> And the haughtiness of man shall be humbled,
>   and the pride of men shall be brought low;
>   and the Lord alone will be exalted in that day (Isa. 2:12,17).

The attempts of man to escape will prove to be futile. Neither Sheol, the deepest point imaginable, nor the heavens, as high above as Sheol was deep, would provide a way of escape. For,

> Though they dig into Sheol,
>   from there shall my hand take them;
>   though they climb up to heaven,
>   from there I will bring them down (9:2).

Men may travel to the mountain peaks or go to the bottom of the sea, but judgment cannot be averted. Amos continued:

> Though they hide themselves on the top of Carmel,
>   for there I will search out and take them;
> and though they hide from my sight at the bottom of the sea,
>   there I will command the serpent, and it shall bite them (9:3).

Carmel was an example of inaccessibility, says Harper, "not only for its height (1800 ft. above the sea), but more especially for its limestone caves (said to exceed 2000 in number, and to be so close together and so serpentine as to make the discovery of a fugitive entirely impossible), and its forests, which in the days of Strabo, . . . were the retreat of robbers."[3]

Reference to the serpent reflects the ancient Near Eastern belief concerning the great serpent of the sea. Welch states that "the serpent in the sea-bottom may once have been a rival power to the God of order; but Amos is able to speak of it and use it in his prophecy, because already the Hebrew faith has outgrown the risk of his reference to the sea-serpent being misunderstood."[4] An examination of other Old Testament references will reveal overtones of a conflict between Yahweh of Israel and the serpent of chaos (cf. Job 26:13; Psalm 74:13-14; 89:9-10; Isa. 51:9). Also, the personification of evil under the figure of the serpent became familiar to apocalyptic writers (Isa. 27:1), and the eventual New Testament usage of the figure (Rev. 12:9-15; 20:2) roots far back into the remote and hidden past of Israel's Mesopotamian origins. The point which Amos sought to emphasize was that no place lay beyond the power of God's control, not even the bottom of the sea.

A third alternative was suggested by Amos: "Suppose the nation goes into captivity, will not life in a foreign land take them beyond God's judgment?" To this hypothetical question Amos answered:

> Though they go into captivity before their enemies,
>   there I will command the sword, and it shall slay them;
> and I will set my eyes upon them
>   for evil and not for good (9:4).

According to the common belief of the day, God was limited to the land of Israel (cf. Jonah; David, 1 Sam. 26:19-20; Naaman, 2 Kings 5:15-17), and many felt that if they could but leave the land, God would be left behind. Amos broke with this traditional view that localized God, emphasizing that man could not escape God no matter what he might do. Even in a captivity which took

---

[3] *Op. cit.,* p. 189.

[4] Adam C. Welch, *The Religion of Israel Under the Kingdom* (Edinburgh: T. & T. Clark, 1912), p. 70.

man away from the land, God was present. No man can travel so far or hide so cleverly as to escape the judgment of God. Wherever the reality of man's sin appears, judgment cannot be far behind.

Judgment is irresistible, 9:5-6.—Modern man has sought to make God in his own image and in so doing has become his own god. In this self-deluded state of divinity he feels that he can create his own destiny. Any suggestion of divine judgment or retribution in history is immediately rejected on at least two bases. First, modern man by and large has denied the reality of sin as rebellion against God. Second, modern man insists that through scientific technology, social progress, and a host of other aids, the future can be determined by the power of man himself. Nothing could be more absurd. Amos would never have accepted such insinuations, as do many modern prophets. In the prophet's own day he stressed the irresistible nature of judgment.

The action of God revealed the irresistible nature of judgment (9:5-6c). In a vivid description of God's action on earth, which cannot be pressed in every literal detail, Amos saw such power as to convince him that judgment was irresistible. The Lord was one

> who touches the earth and it melts,
>   and all who dwell in it mourn,
> and all of it rises like the Nile,
>   and sinks again, like the Nile of Egypt (9:5).

He causes the earth to melt (probably reflecting either volcanic activity or an extreme metaphor for drought), brings such consternation to the people as to produce a state of mourning, and produces convulsions upon the earth so that it "rises" and "sinks" like the Nile (reflecting, again, the earthquake in the second year of the prophets ministry). One whose action on earth is unlimited, is quite capable of judgment which will be irresistible in its ultimate manifestation.

Not only in his earthly action but in the cosmic action of God as well, the power of an irresistible might was revealed. Amos could speak of God as one

> who builds his upper chambers in the heavens,
>   and founds his vault upon the earth;

who calls for the waters of the sea,
and pours them out upon the surface of the earth—
the Lord is his name (9:6).

The ancient Hebrew's view of the universe was considerably
different from that of the modern space age. His view was that
the third story of the universe constituted the dwelling of God.
There, in the "heaven of heavens," God had built his upper cham-
bers, said the prophet Amos. Beneath this was the vault of heaven,
or firmament, which separated "the waters which were under the
firmament from the waters which were above the firmament" (Gen.
1:7). The Hebrew thus conceived of the sky as an inverted bowl,
or vault, stretching from one horizon to another in a complete
circle. One who could so establish his dwellings and set the vault
upon the rim of the earth was, indeed, irresistible in power.

Not only was the very construction of the heavens and the vault
a miracle of God's power, but the treatment of the water as well.
God had but "to call for the waters of the sea" and they came at
his bidding. Once before his presence, he poured them out as rain
upon the surface of the earth. Meteorologically, this is not an absolutely adequate explanation for the rain. Theologically, it is valid
today just as it was in the time of Amos, for it places emphasis
upon the controlling power of God, despite the methodology involved in producing rain. Whether by evaporation, condensation,
or whatever physical means, the fact remains abidingly true that
it is of God. Modern science has produced explanations for many
of the phenomena of life, and in the process has removed much
of the mystery inherent in the universe during the time of Amos.
Yet, despite man's understanding, there runs a divine mystery
through all of the universe that defies total comprehension.

The universe is no longer viewed as one of "three stories":
earth, sky, and home of the gods. Yet, in the process, the breadth
of God's nature remains such as to encompass even the expanding
universe of modern scientific thought, without reducing the
stature of God. The solution to a changing view of the universe
does not lie in the perpetuation of a "little" science which will not
dwarf God. Rather, the solution lies in the recognition of the sheer
immensity of God, who is transcendent to the point of embracing
even an "expanding universe." Modern science, rather than de-
stroying faith, increases its depth as it portrays the magnitude of

what God has done in his created order. One can say in the space age with even greater wonder than the psalmist, "When I consider thy heavens, the work of thy fingers, the moon and the stars, which thou hast ordained; what is man, that thou art mindful of him?" (Psalm 8:3-4a, KJV).

Judgment is indiscriminate, 9:7-8a.—Discrimination is an issue relevant to the totality of the twentieth-century world. Whether it be racial, social, economic, or political discrimination, the very word itself need only be spoken in order to divide any group into two divisions. Amos confronted a similar problem in his day, for Israel felt that God had some special concern for her that he did not have for others. Because of this discriminatory attitude, Israel felt that even the judgment of God could be averted. In opposition to this attitude, Amos insisted that judgment is always indiscriminate.

The premise on which Amos built his case for the indiscriminate nature of judgment centered in the fact that Israel was just like any other people. Amos pricked the bubble of Israel's pride and arrogance by saying, "'Are you not like the Ethiopians to me, O people of Israel?' says the Lord" (9:7a). The Ethiopians of Nubia were noted for their dark skins, says Robinson (cf. Jer. 13:23), and were so despised.[5] One wonders if Amos was any more popular in his day than the modern preacher who might rise and say to the twentieth-century America, "Are you not like the black men—the Negroes—to me, O people of America, says the Lord." Whether the average individual liked it or not, this was the premise of Amos' argument.

The astounding illustration of Amos' premise lay in the fact that God had brought up other nations, even as he had brought up Israel. The most hated of Israel's enemies, the Philistines and the Syrians or Aramaeans, had been under God's guidance even as had Israel. Israel need not feel any sense of superiority, for "Did I not bring up Israel from the land of Egypt, and the Philistines from Caphtor and the Syrians from Kir?" (9:7b). The question needed no answer; the answer was obvious.

The conclusion to the argument of Amos was clear. If Yahweh had acted so indiscriminately in the past, he would continue to do so. His character would never change. Because of his univer-

---

[5] "Amos," *op. cit.*, p. 783.

sality and his indiscriminate nature, God's judgment would fall upon Israel since she was like all other nations in his eyes. As Amos expressed it, "Behold, the eyes of the Lord God are upon the sinful kingdom, and I will destroy it from the surface of the ground" (9:8a). In this assertion Amos made two significant contributions. First, God evaluates indiscriminately: "The eyes of the Lord God are upon the sinful kingdom." No man need ever believe that he is beyond God's notice and evaluation. The medieval architect and artist who introduced the "all-seeing eye" into church architecture captured a vital truth about the character of God. His eye is upon man's every action.

Second, God not only evaluates indiscriminately, but he destroys in the same manner. Concerning the kingdom of Israel, the Lord said, "I will destroy it from the surface of the ground." If God destroyed Israel without discrimination, why should any nation conceive itself to be immune from destruction? Destruction comes without discrimination. Nation, society, or individual, each must bear a destruction that is without discrimination.

Modern man thinks of the judgment of God as something repulsive and, therefore, to be rejected. His judgment is to be feared of course. Yet, there is something worse than God's judgment—a god who could see sin and degeneracy throughout society, insincerity and hypocrisy in religion, and do nothing about either. Even as judgment falls, voices should rise heavenward in praise and recognition of a God who speaks! This is man's end—the judgment of God: inevitable, inescapable, irresistible, and indiscriminate. But this need not be the absolute end, it can be God's new beginning.

God's New Beginning, 9:8b-15

Is it possible that "the end" is not the end at all? Is it conceivable that this end spawned by judgment in history is but the new beginning? Could it be that judgment within the framework of history is redemptive in that it confronts man with sufficient motivation to lead him back to God, who will heal and restore the fellowship broken by sin? In the mind of the prophets, the "end" was always but the opportunity for God's new beginning. "The end" never terminated history in prophetic thought. The events portrayed after judgment and chastisement were set in a renovated and purged land, to be sure, but the same land and the same people with whom God had dealt all along. In a very real sense, the prophetic "end" was but God's new beginning.

The message of doom pronounced by the prophet was alleviated by one of hope found in the concluding verses of the book. While Amos 9:8b-15 may well be the work of one subsequent to the ministry of Amos, it should be approached from the point of view that it represents the purposes of God to restore his people following the Exile, regardless of authorship. Even though the matter of authorship should be considered frankly and honestly, at the same time it must be understood that authorship does not affect the validity of the relevatory nature of the passage. Whether the passage came from Amos or a subsequent writer does not affect adversely the intentions of God on behalf of his people. Regardless of its source of authorship, the passage represented Israel's ultimate understanding of the purpose of God concerning her destiny.

From doom to discipline, 9:8b-10.—Judgment may be viewed, as may any other experience, from two opposite poles. It may be considered from the positive side, in which case the emphasis will be placed upon the corrective and chastening side of judgment. On the other hand, it may be viewed as retributive and penal in nature, with no purpose other than the punishment of the guilty culprit. Amos was led of God to emphasize that judgment for Israel moved from a sense of doom to one of discipline.

Destruction in the ultimate sense was denied quite strongly by the prophet (9:8b). Although the earlier part of verse 8 had stated that God would "destroy it [the nation] from the surface of the ground," the latter part of the verse tempered this by indicating, "except that I will not utterly destroy the house of Jacob." The judgment of God is always tempered by mercy, stressed Amos. As Hosea also emphasized, "I will not execute my fierce anger, I will not again destroy Ephraim; for I am God and not man, the Holy One in your midst, and I will not come to destroy" (11:9).

The judgment of God throughout the Old Testament is for the purpose of "bringing man to his senses." It is never merely retributive in nature. This element of grace and mercy which appears even in judgment can be traced, as Hosea said, to the fact that God is God and not man. The judgment of man is oftentimes only uncontrolled anger and rage. With God, wrath is never uncontrolled. Indeed, it is highly controlled and administered, all for the purpose of bringing such pressures to bear upon man that his life can be made to conform to the will and purpose of God.

Discipline by exile was described for Israel. "For lo," said the Lord, "I will command, and shake the house of Israel among all the nations as one shakes with a sieve" (9:9). Either the exile of the Northern Kingdom in the late eighth century or the exile of Judah in the early sixth century was envisioned by the author (depending upon whether or not one attributes the passage to eighth-century Amos). In either instance, the nation was to be scattered as when a sieve is used.

The phrase, "but no pebble shall fall upon the ground," has been variously interpreted. The word translated at times "grain" is *tsᵉrōr*, but is better understood as "pebble" as in the Revised Standard Version translation. Cripps has made an extensive study of the precise methodology involved in the passage and has concluded that the message is essentially one of doom for Israel.[6]

It has been argued that the good grain is to be kept in the sieve, allowing the chaff to fall upon the ground. Arguments have ranged over whether the author intended (1) a small sieve, holding the grain but allowing the chaff to fall; (2) a large corn sieve which allowed the grain to fall, but kept out the rocks that were then destroyed (as at an old-fashioned "gristmill" which kept out pieces of corn cob and other debris); or (3) a sand-sieve used in sifting sand in order to separate the sand and the pebbles (which would fit well the true meaning of *tsᵉrōr*).

Although the reversal of what one would expect, it seems best to understand the pebble as the "good" in Israel that Yahweh would keep, since it seems that he is contrasting those who have known judgment by being shaken among all the nations with those who have been preserved from such a fate. "But no pebble shall fall upon the earth" would be, in effect, "but none that I have held back shall suffer such a fate." This was certainly the attitude which prevailed by the time of Malachi (cf. Mal. 3:17 to 4:3).[7]

In either instance, the prophet stressed that the exile would be a time of separation and of evaluation. Beyond this the figure of

[6] *Op. cit.*, pp. 265-68.
[7] *Ibid.*, p. 268.

speech should not be pressed. Normally, a figure of speech or an analogy has one primary point of emphasis. Errors of interpretation may often be traced to the effort to make every facet of an analogy teach some specific truth. In Amos 9:9 the prophet simply emphasized separation and evaluation, nothing more than this should be attached to the verse. Even the exile could be a time of discipline through separation. Thus, the prophet underscored the truth that doom can be turned to discipline.

The doom of sinners was decreed on the part of all within the nation (9:10). The doom of the sinner was the result of the separation mentioned in 9:9. In making this emphasis, the prophet underscored the *inclusiveness* of judgment by saying, "All the sinners of my people shall die by the sword" (9:10*a*). God is not arbitrary, and even those of his own people who have sinned will be destroyed. No generation can validly anticipate favoritism when retribution falls.

The insolence which characterized Israel had brought about their inclusion within the framework of judgment, said the prophet. Surrounded by sin in its every manifestation, they could say, "Evil shall not overtake us" (9:10*b*). This is the constant cry of respectability. It insists that "nothing is really wrong; nothing is going to happen." Insolence that can deny the principle of moral retribution must always "die by the sword." To deny this is either to deny the morality or the sovereignty of God.

From humiliation to exaltation, 9:11-12.—From such a time of humiliation as that which accompanied the Exile, Israel was to be led into an era of exaltation. Kirkpatrick has observed:

Amos has no prediction of a personal Messiah. But it is noteworthy that he does connect the hope of the future with the house of David. This is to be restored to its pristine glory, and through its restoration blessing comes to the reunited nation which exercises a sovereignty over surrounding nations as of old.[8]

The rebuilding of the fallen people was described in the following words,

"In that day I will raise up
the booth of David that is fallen

---

[8] *Op. cit.*, p. 103.

and repair its breaches,
and raise up its ruins,
and rebuild it as in the days of old;
that they may possess the remnant of Edom
and all the nations who are called by my name,"
says the Lord who does this (9:11-12).

The use of the term "booth" of David is indicative of the low state
of the Davidic line. Robinson observes that "it denoted a rough shel-
ter for cattle (Gen. 33:17), for soldiers on campaign (2 Sam. 11:11),
for watchers in vineyards (Isa. 1:8)."[9] This stood in marked contrast to the glory of Jerusalem prior to her destruction. All of this
was to be changed radically by the transforming power of God. The
last deed had not been performed and the writer insisted that the
fallen booth of David would be raised, its broken walls repaired,
its ruins renovated. It would be rebuilt in accordance with the glory
of its former position. All of this would be accompanied by the re-
possession of the land, for "they may possess the remnant of Edom
and all the nations who are called by my name" (9:12). Such statements of the prophet shall be understood, however, in the light of
Kirkpatrick's observation that Amos "is still the representative of
a rudimentary stage of prophetic revelation, to be enlarged, developed, spiritualized by his successors; to be fulfilled, not indeed
in the letter, but in the spirit." [10]

The responsibility for such action lay in the power of God, for
the prophet concluded by saying, "says the Lord who does this"
(9:12b). By this assertion he disclaimed any automatic process
inherent in society that would bring about its redemption. Although
God does utilize forces inherent in history and society, these are
always subordinate to him and are often only the expression of his
character. The hope of man, said the writer, was not around him
but above him. When these two forces, those around and those
from above, are properly related one to another, man's redemption
is made possible. But it requires the action of a God who acts in
history, not One who ignores either history or society.

From privation to plenty, 9:13-15.—The prophets of the Old
Testament often depicted the future blessedness of man's fellowship

---

[9] "Amos," *op. cit.*, p. 783.
[10] *Op. cit.*, p. 103.

with God through the symbol of a renovated natural order. The earth was felt to share in the fate of man. In man's sin, nature also suffered. "Cursed is the ground because of you; . . . thorns and thistles it shall bring forth to you" (Gen. 3:17-18). Paul could speak of the creation as waiting

with eager longing for the revealing of the sons of God; for the creation was subjected to futility, not of its own will but by the will of him who subjected it in hope; because the creation itself will be set free from its bondage to decay and obtain the glorious liberty of the children of God. We know that the whole creation has been groaning in travail together until now; and not only the creation, but we ourselves (Rom. 8:19-23).

According to biblical thought patterns, the earth also shared in the joy of man's redemption. Consequently, the Old Testament prophets depicted the unique transformation of earth as an attendant phenomenon of the redemptive action of God. Isaiah could speak of the time when "the wolf shall dwell with the lamb, and the leopard shall lie down the kid, . . . the lion and the fatling together, and a little child shall lead them" (11:6). The same book could depict the blossoming of the desert (35:1) and say,

> the burning sand shall become a pool,
>   and the thirsty ground springs of water;
> the haunt of jackals shall become a swamp,
>   the grass shall become reeds and rushes (35:7).

Ezekiel symbolized this same era by referring to a time when the entire area of the Dead Sea would be renovated (cf. Ezek. 47:1 ff.).

Such statements do not necessarily indicate a literal transformation of the earth. Two examples of fulfilment are: First, reference was made in Isaiah 40:1-5 to the preparation made for the return of God's people. The prophet of the Exile said,

> A voice cries:
> "In the wilderness prepare the way of the Lord,
>   make straight in the desert a highway for our God.
> Every valley shall be lifted up,
>   and every mountain and hill be made low;
> the uneven ground shall become level,
>   and the rough places a plain" (40:3-4).

The New Testament makes reference to this experience (Mark 1:2-3) and assumes that it was fulfilled in the time of John the Baptist's ministry (cf. Mark 1:4 ff). Although the principle of Isaiah 40:1 ff. found its fulfilment in the ministry and time of John, there was never a time when, literally, the valleys were lifted up, every mountain made low, and the rough places plain.

Second, Joel described the redemptive era of God's purpose by saying,

> And it shall come to pass afterward,
>   that I will pour out my spirit on all flesh;
> your sons and your daughters shall prophesy,
>   your old men shall dream dreams,
>   and your young men shall see visions.
> Even upon the menservants and maidservants
>   in those days, I will pour out my spirit.
> And I will give portents in the heavens and on the earth, blood and fire and columns of smoke. The sun shall be turned to darkness, and the moon to blood, before the great and terrible day of the Lord comes (2:28-31).

At the time of the coming of the Holy Spirit, direct reference was made to this statement of Joel. The Apostle Peter explained the unusual conduct of the people by saying, "these men are not drunk, as you suppose, since it is only the third hour of the day; but this is what was spoken by the prophet Joel" (Acts 2:15-16).

In these two instances, Old Testament prophecies were viewed by New Testament authority to have been fulfilled in spirit. Yet, the attendant physical phenomena were not recorded. Obviously they did not accompany the fulfilment of the principle, or real content of the prophecy. This does not invalidate the prophetic ministry of the prophets. Rather, it illustrates that the physical descriptions were literary devices used to express a truth that otherwise would have defied description.

In passages such as Amos 9:13-15 it was never intended that the physical descriptions were to be made the heart of the prophecy. The prophet sought by this means to express the blessing of God as man understood it in his day. The method of expressing the bliss of God's redemptive order may change from one era to another. The reality of that divine redemption, on the other hand, never changes; it remains as one unchanging factor in a changing universe.

It is against such an explanatory background as this that Amos 9:13-15 must be considered, reading the passage with a sense of poetic sensitivity and identification with the original writer. Hear Amos as he describes the wonder of God's redeemed, re-created order:

> "Behold, the days are coming," says the Lord
>   "when the plowman shall overtake the reaper
>   and the treader of grapes him who sows the seed;
> the mountains shall drip sweet wine,
>   and all the hills shall flow with it.
> I will restore the fortunes of my people Israel,
>   and they shall rebuild the ruined cities and inhabit them;
> they shall plant vineyards and drink their wine,
>   and they shall make gardens and eat their fruit.
> I will plant them upon their land,
>   and they shall never again be plucked up
>   out of the land which I have given them,"
>   says the Lord your God (9:13-15).

Amos thus emphasized that Israel would know the return of numerous and plenteous harvests (9:13), the rebuilding of destroyed cities (9:-14a), the replanting of vineyards (9:14b), and the re-establishment of Israel upon her own land (9:15). In all of this the prophet sought to express, in words that his hearers could comprehend, the inexpressible wonder of Israel's future as fellowship with God was attained as never before in her history. The reality of such fellowship, however, was definitely not to be predicated upon the literal fulfilment of the physical side of the prophecy.

The startling reality of man's end is alleviated considerably by the understanding that such an end may be only God's new beginning. Herein lies the hope of contemporary social and religious structures. Destined to an inevitable end by the fruit of their own self-will and rebellion, religious structures may find that the end of their present, institutionalized structure may be but the opportunity for God to make a new beginning. Both individually and collectively, this constitutes the hope of the current social and religious crisis: man's end can be God's new beginning.

Bibliography

ALINGTON, C. A. *A New Approach to the Old Testament*. London: G. Bell & Sons, 1937.

ANDERSON, BERNHARD W. *Understanding the Old Testament*. Englewood Cliffs, N.J.: Prentice-Hall, 1957.

ANDERSON, GEORGE W. *A Critical Introduction to the Old Testament*. London: Gerald Duckworth & Co., 1959.

BAAB, OTTO J. *Prophetic Preaching: A New Approach*. New York: Abingdon Press, 1958.

BAER, DALLAS C. *The Message of the Prophets to Their Day and Ours*. Great Neck, N.Y.: Pulpit Digest Publishing Co., 1940.

BARTH, KARL. *The Epistle to the Romans*. Translated by EDWYN C. HOSKYNS. London: Oxford University Press, 1953.

BENTZEN, AAGE. *Introduction to the Old Testament*. 2 vols. Copenhagen: G. E. C. Gad Publisher, 1949.

BLACKWOOD, ANDREW W. *Preaching from Prophetic Books*. New York: Abingdon-Cokesbury Press, 1951.

BLANK, SHELDON H. *Prophetic Faith in Isaiah*. New York: Harper & Bros., 1958.

BRIGHT, JOHN. *A History of Israel*. Philadelphia: The Westminster Press, 1959.

_____. *The Kingdom of God*. New York: Abingdon-Cokesbury Press, 1953.

BROWN, FRANCIS, DRIVER, S. R., and BRIGGS, CHARLES A. *A Hebrew and English Lexicon of the Old Testament*. Oxford: The Clarendon Press, 1959.

BRUNNER, EMIL. *The Letter to the Romans*. Philadelphia: The Westminster Press, 1959.

BUBER, MARTIN. *The Prophetic Faith*. New York: Harper & Bros., 1960.

CALKINS, RAYMOND. *The Modern Message of the Minor Prophets*. New York: Harper & Bros., 1947.

CRIPPS, RICHARD S. (ed.). *A Critical and Exegetical Commentary on the Book of Amos*. 2d ed. London: S.P.C.K., 1955.

COHON, BERYL D. *The Prophets.* New York: Bloch Publishing Co., 1960.

DAVIES, G. HENTON, WALLIS, CHARLES L., and RICHARDSON, ALAN (eds.). "Amos," *The Twentieth Century Bible Commentary.* rev. ed. New York: Harper & Bros., 1956.

DEERE, DERWARD WILLIAM. *The Twelve Speak.* Vol. I. New York: The American Press, 1958.

DRIVER, S. R. *The Books of Joel and Amos.* ("The Cambridge Bible Series.") Cambridge: The University Press, 1915.

EDGHILL, ERNEST ARTHUR. *The Book of Amos.* 2d ed. London: Methuen & Co., 1914.

EISELEN, FREDERICK CARL. *Prophecy and the Prophets in Their Historical Relations.* New York: The Methodist Book Concern, 1909.

ELMSLIE, W. A. L. *How Came Our Faith.* New York: Charles Scribner's Sons, 1949.

FAUS, W. ARTHUR. *The Genius of the Prophets.* New York: Abingdon-Cokesbury Press, 1946.

FOSBROKE, HUGHELL E. W. "Amos," *The Interpreter's Bible.* Vol. VI. New York: Abingdon Press, 1956.

FRANCISCO, CLYDE T. *Introducing the Old Testament.* Nashville: Broadman Press, 1950.

GOLDBERG, DAVID. *Meet the Prophets.* ed. LEONARD R. SUSSMAN. New York: Bookman Associates, 1956.

GORDON, ALEX R. *The Prophets of the Old Testament.* New York: George H. Doran Co., 1916.

GOTTWALD, NORMAN K. *A Light to the Nations: An Introduction to the Old Testament.* New York: Harper & Bros., 1959.

_____. *Studies in the Book of Lamentations.* London: SCM Press, 1954.

GWYNN, R. M. (ed.). *The Book of Amos.* Cambridge: The University Press, 1927.

HARPER, W. R. *A Critical and Exegetical Commentary on Amos and Hosea.* ("The International Critical Commentary.") Edinburgh: T. & T. Clark, 1953.

HASTINGS, EDWARD (ed.). *The Minor Prophets.* ("The Speaker's Bible.") Scotland: The Speaker's Bible Office, 1930.

HASTINGS, JAMES (ed.). *The Greater Men and Women of the Bible.* 6 vols. New York: Charles Scribner's Sons, 1913-16.

HEINISCH, PAUL. *Theology of the Old Testament.* Collegeville, Minn.: The Liturgical Press, 1950.

HEIM, KARL. *Christian Faith and Natural Science.* New York: Harper & Bros., 1953.

HESCHEL, ABRAHAM J. *The Prophets of Israel.* New York: Harper & Row, 1962.

HORTON, R. F. (ed.). *The Minor Prophets: Hosea, Joel, Amos, Obadiah, Jonah, and Micah* ("The Century Bible.") Edinburgh: T. & T. Clark and E. C. Jack, n.d.

HYATT, J. PHILLIP. *Prophetic Religion*. New York: Abingdon-Cokesbury Press, 1947.

JAMES, FLEMING. *Personalities of the Old Testament*. New York: Charles Scribner's Sons, 1939.

KAPELRUD, ARVID S. "God as Destroyer in the Preaching of Amos and in the Ancient Near East," *Journal of Biblical Literature* (Philadelphia), (March, 1952).

KENT, CHARLES FOSTER and SMITH, ROBERT SENECA. *The Work and Teachings of the Earlier Prophets*. New York: Young Men's Christian Association Press, 1907.

KIRKPATRICK, A. F. *The Doctrine of the Prophets*. 3d ed. London: Macmillan & Co., 1917.

KNIGHT, GEORGE A. F. *Hosea*. London: SCM Press, 1960.

KNUDSON, ALBERT C. *The Beacon Lights of Prophecy*. New York: The Methodist Book Concern, 1914.

KUHL, CURT. *The Prophets of Israel*. Translated by RUDOLF J. EHRLICH and J. P. SMITH. Edinburgh: Oliver & Boyd, 1960.

LEHRMAN, S. M. "Amos," *The Twelve Prophets*. Edited by A. COHEN. Bournemouth: The Soncino Press, 1948.

LESLIE, ELMER A. *The Prophets Tell Their Own Story*. New York: Abingdon Press, 1939.

LUTHI, WALTER. *In the Time of Earthquake*. Translated by H. L. M. HAIRE and IAN HENDERSON. London: Hodder & Stoughton, 1940.

MACARTNEY, CLARENCE EDWARD. *Chariots of Fire and Other Sermons on Bible Characters*. New York: Abingdon-Cokesbury Press, 1951.

MACLAREN, ALEXANDER. *The Books of Ezekiel, Daniel, and the Minor Prophets*. ("Expositions of Holy Scripture," Vol. VI.) Grand Rapids: Wm. B. Erdmans Publishing Co., 1959.

McCOWN, CHESTER CHARLTON. *The Ladder of Progress in Palestine*. New York: Harper & Bros., 1943.

MARNEY, CARLYLE. *Faith in Conflict*. New York: Abingdon Press, 1957.

MARSH, JOHN. *Amos and Micah*. ("Torch Series.") London: SCM Press, 1959.

MATTUCK, ISRAEL I. *The Thought of the Prophets*. London: George Allen & Unwin, 1953.

McFADYEN, JOHN EDGAR. *A Cry for Justice: A Study in Amos*. Edited by JOHN ADAMS. ("The Short Course Series.") New York: Charles Scribner's Sons, 1912.

_____. *The Use of the Old Testament*. London: James Clark & Co., n.d.

MILLER, MADELEINE S. and J. LANE. "Amos," *Harper's Bible Dictionary.* New York: Harper & Bros., 1952.

MILLEY, C. ROSS. *The Prophets of Israel.* New York: Philosophical Library, 1959.

MILTON, JOHN P. *Prophecy Interpreted.* Minneapolis: Augsburg Publishing House, 1960.

MITCHELL, H. G. *Amos: An Essay in Exegesis.* rev. ed. Boston: Houghton, Mifflin & Co., 1900.

MORGAN, G. CAMPBELL. *Living Messages of the Books of the Bible.* Westwood, N.J.: Fleming H. Revell Co., 1960.

_____. *The Minor Prophets.* Westwood, N.J.: Fleming H. Revell Co., 1960.

NORTH, CHRISTOPHER R. *The Old Testament Interpretation of History.* London: The Epworth Press, 1946.

OESTERLEY, W. O. E. and ROBINSON, T. H. *An Introduction to the Books of the Old Testament.* ("Living Age Books.") New York: Meridian Books, 1934.

OTTLEY, R. L. *The Hebrew Prophets.* ("Oxford Church Text Books.") 4th ed. London: Rivingtons, 1898.

PATERSON, JOHN. *The Goodly Fellowship of the Prophets.* New York: Charles Scribner's Sons, 1949.

PFEIFFER, ROBERT H. *Introduction to the Old Testament.* rev. ed. New York: Harper & Bros., 1948.

PHILLIPS, J. B. *Your God Is Too Small.* New York: The Macmillan Co., 1956.

PRITCHARD, JAMES B. *Ancient Near Eastern Texts Relating to the Old Testament.* Princeton, N.J.: Princeton University Press, 1950.

ROBINSON, H. WHEELER. "Amos," *The Abingdon Bible Commentary.* Edited by FREDERICK C. EISELSEN, EDWIN LEWIS and DAVID G. DOWNEY. New York: The Abingdon Press, 1929.

_____. *The Cross in the Old Testament.* London: SCM Press, 1955.

_____. *Inspiration and Revelation in the Old Testament.* Oxford: At the Clarendon Press, 1946.

_____. *Redemption and Revelation in the Actuality of History.* New York: Harper & Bros., 1942.

ROBINSON, THEODORE H. *Prophecy and the Prophets in Ancient Israel.* New York: Charles Scribner's Sons, 1923.

ROWLEY, H. H. *The Biblical Doctrine of Election.* London: Lutterworth Press, 1950.

_____. *The Growth of the Old Testament.* London: Hutchinson's University Library, 1950.

Rust, E. C. "Old Testament Theology." Louisville, Ky.: Southern Baptist Theological Seminary, 1953. (Mimeographed.)

Skinner, John. *Prophecy and Religion*. Cambridge: Cambridge University Press, 1922.

Smart, J. D. "Amos," *The Interpreter's Dictionary of the Bible*. 4 vols. New York: Abingdon Press, 1962.

Smith, George Adam. *The Book of the Twelve Prophets*. rev. ed. 2 vols. Garden City: Doubleday, Doran & Co., 1929.

Smith, J. M. Powis. *The Prophet and His Problems*. New York: Charles Scribner's Sons, 1916.

——. *The Prophets and Their Times*. 2d ed. Chicago: The University of Chicago Press, 1941.

Smith, Roy L. *The Bible and the First World State*. ("Know Your Bible Series," No. 2.) New York: Abingdon-Cokesbury Press, 1943.

Smith, W. Robertson. *The Prophets of Israel and Their Place in History*. 2d ed. London: Adam & Charles Black, 1902.

Snaith, Norman H. *Amos, Hosea and Micah*. ("Epworth Preacher's Commentaries.") London: The Epworth Press, 1956.

Sutcliffe, T. H. *The Book of Amos*. London: S.P.C.K., 1939.

Taylor, J. "Amos," *A Dictionary of the Bible*. Vol. I. Edited by James Hastings. New York: Charles Scribner's Sons, 1908.

Tregelles, Samuel Prideaux. *Gesenius' Hebrew and Chaldee Lexicon*. Grand Rapids: Wm. B. Eerdmans Publishing Co., 1957.

Trueblood, Elton. *The Predicament of Modern Man*. New York: Harper & Bros., 1944.

Voegelin, Eric. *Israel and Revelation*. ("Order and History Series," Vol. I.) Baton Rouge: Louisiana State University Press, 1956.

Watts, John D. W. *Vision and Prophecy in Amos*. Grand Rapids: Wm. B. Eerdmans Publishing Co., 1958.

Welch, Adam C. *The Religion of Israel Under the Kingdom*. Edinburgh: T. & T. Clark, 1912.

Wellhausen, Julius. *Prolegomena to the History of Ancient Israel*. New York: Meridian Books, 1957.

Weston, Sidney A. *The Prophets and the Problems of Life*. Philadelphia: The Westminster Press, 1932.

Willett, Herbert L. *The Prophets of Israel*. ("Bethany C. E. Reading Courses.") New York: Fleming H. Revell Co., 1899.

Williams, Walter G. *The Prophets: Pioneers to Christianity*. New York: Abingdon Press, 1956.

Wilson, Dorothy Clarke. *The Herdsman*. Philadelphia: The Westminster Press, 1946.

Wolfe, Rolland Emerson. *Meet Amos and Hosea, the Prophets of Israel*. New York: Harper & Bros., 1945.